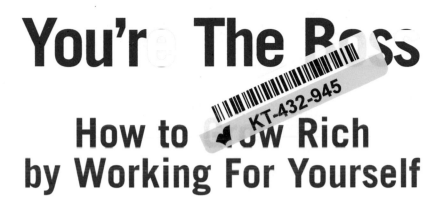

You're The Boss

How to Grow Rich
by Working For Yourself

Mike Lipkin   Eric Parker

Touch The Sky Publishers

Cape Town Johannesburg Toronto

Copyright 1999 by Mike Lipkin and Eric Parker
First edition in 1999 by Touch The Sky Publishers
16 Castle Street, Fellside, Johannesburg
Cover Photograph by Peter Baasch
Cartoons by Charl Bruwer
Reproduction by KCB Typesetting
Printed and bound by Supreme Printers
PO Box 11116, Johannesburg 2000

SBN 0-620-24047-4

Contents

Acknowledgements

This book was conceptualized, written and printed at turbo speed. It would not have been possible without the commitment and rapid action of some very special people.

Firstly, we want to thank Deloitte & Touche for believing in us and supporting this book. Specifically, we want to thank Vassi Naidoo and Charles Godfrey for their trust and partnership.

We would also like to thank all the Franchisors and service providers who shared our vision and responded to our invitation to participate in this book. Specifically, we would like to thank ABSA, Baby Boom, Butterfield Bread, Debonairs Pizza, DM Kisch Inc, King Pie, Kleins, Liberty Life, Nando's, Nizams, Multiserv, PG Autoglass, Pick 'n Pay Franchise, Pleasure Foods, Postnet, Spec-Savers and Spur Steak Ranches.

We are grateful to Anita du Toit for her insight, groundwork and "it's never a problem" attitude.

We could never have made this book happen without Giuli and Vivien from Giuli Osso Communications. They made the impossible possible.

We also want to thank Lesley-Caren Johnson for her highly useful pre-business checklist listed in Appendix 1.

Charl Bruwer was also amazing in his ability to interpret the spirit of the book through his ingenious cartoons.

We are grateful to Terry Lamb from KCB Typesetting and Supreme Printers who was instrumental in making this book happen.

Finally, we want to thank you for buying this book. You are the reason for all our endeavours. Enjoy and prosper!

Foreword by Vassi Naidoo, CEO Deloitte & Touche South Africa

At Deloitte & Touche, our four core values are strength from cultural diversity, service, commitment to each other and integrity. That's why we are delighted to be associated with this important book. We want to put our values into action to the benefit of the country and, specifically, to the benefit of the thousands of entrepreneurs who represent this country's future.

We know there can be no true democracy without economic empowerment. And, like everywhere else in the world, economic empowerment is ultimately in the hands of small business people and emerging entrepreneurs. That's why Deloitte & Touche is deeply involved in the development of small business and entrepreneurs. Our Entrepreneurial Services Division and Business Beat initiative take our expertise directly to grass roots level.

As one of the major professional services companies in South Africa, we have a powerful commitment to help shape this country's future. South Africa has been extremely good to us. We believe we have to put back more than we've taken out. That's why we will do everything in our power to create opportunities and jobs. Investing in this book is just another way of walking our talk.

Mike Lipkin has worked with Deloitte & Touche all over the world. I believe he has the energy, the commitment and the ability to help empower small businesspeople and entrepreneurs to achieve their dreams. Eric Parker is an associate of mine at Deloitte & Touche where he heads up the Franchising Consulting Division. I know that both Mike and Eric share my desire to make a difference by giving South Africans both the motivation and the skills to empower themselves.

Enjoy this book. Use this book. And share its lessons with others. We're only as good as all of us together.

Wanted:

People with courage looking for a little adventure.

Welcome to your glorious future. You've got what it takes!

Congratulations!! You've taken a big step to joining the rare breed of millionaire businesspeople who are living the adventure of their life - independent, motivated and fulfilled.

You see, you've taken action. You've acquired this book. You've made the investment. You've demonstrated your commitment to making it happen unlike the thousands of people in South Africa today who wonder what's happening.

Right up front, we want to promise you one thing: This book is fun. This book will make you smile. This book will make you laugh and it may even make you cry. This book is easy to read. This book is simple but it's content is powerful. This book will help you master yourself, your life, your relationships and, of course, you're own business.

This book will get you excited and then it will show you how to transform your excitement into love and money. All you need is an open mind and a willing heart.

As we travel through this country, we meet so many people who are complaining about how tough life has been to them. They blame their circumstances and other people for their personal problems. Their favourite words are "If only" and "I wish" and "What for?" They watch life pass them by. And like spectators, they criticize everyone and everything. And you know what the tragedy is? They know what they must do but they don't do what they know they must.

Do you know how the dictionary defines the word "power"? Simply, "The ability to act". People who achieve success are people who take action. They are powerful not passive. So if you are a person of action, we'll help you act right. We'll provide you with the direction, the inspiration, the guidance and the tools to achieving your dreams.

Right now, we don't have to tell you about the uncertainty and chaos in the South African economy. We don't have to tell you how fast things are changing. And we don't have to tell you about how hard it is to find a job anymore. But, maybe, what we do have to tell you is that you may not even want a job anymore. Just maybe, the current conditions in South Africa are ideal for making money. Lots of it. Interested? We're just getting started.

In the June 15 1998 issue of Forbes magazine, the highly respected American business magazine, it was reported that 72% of the 400 richest people in America got that way by starting their own businesses. In fact, what they really did was have the guts to invest in their own ability against the odds. However the article goes on to state that becoming an entrepreneur can make you work 18-hour days and play hell with your family life. Not everyone is psychologically strong enough for the challenge. Are you?

That's why the first sentence of this book was "Wanted: People with COURAGE". But you know what? If you feel a little afraid as you read this paragraph, that's okay. Courage is not the absence of fear. It's the determination to act despite your fear. In fact, if you don't feel fear, you're probably more than just a little stupid.

Maybe the most important point we can make in this entire book is: Don't let your fear stand in your way. There are so many people leading lives of unfulfilled ambitions because they didn't take on their fears. Treat these words as a wake-up call. We promise you that you don't want to get to the end of your days and say, "I should have; If only; Why didn't I; I wish I would have".

The Million Rand Questions

Before you read further, answer the following Million Rand Questions:

Do you have a dream to own and run your own business?

Do you have a dream to be all that you believe you were meant to be?

Do you wake up some days with the feeling that you don't want to go where you have to go to earn your daily bread?

Do you sometimes think: There must be more to life than this!

Do you work for someone you don't respect?

Do you look at some of the wealthy people around you and ask yourself what they have that you don't?

Are you wondering what to do next in your life?

Do you feel as though you're stagnating?

Have you given up on life as an employee in a big company?

Do you hate your work?

Would you love to make money doing what you love?

If you answered yes to any of these Million Rand Questions, the time may be right for you to make your move and move out on your own.

Your head could roll soon

And you know what? Even if you think you're entirely comfortable where you are now, your situation could change in an instant. You could be days away from being downsized, outsourced, rationalized or just plain damn fired. Both of us have heard countless stories of heads rolling just when they thought they were screwed on tight. So don't wait for the axe to fall, be proactive. Start anticipating the future right now. Use this book to plan your future even if your future seems guaranteed (The only thing that's guaranteed is that no-one lives forever. So make the moment count).

After reading what we're about to share with you, we promise you that you'll agree: Working for a boss is really economic slavery designed to keep you permanently in debt.

As a corporate employee, you limit your lifetime income to around R4.8million no matter how hard you work. That assumes 480 pay days (40 years x 12 months), no inflation, and R10000, after tax income at today's value.

Now that may sound like a lot, but look at the opposite side of the balance sheet - your spending. Let's look at a moderate spending pattern over a 40 year period (at today's prices):

PERSONAL INCOME AND EXPENDITURE

INCOME   R4 800 000

EXPENDITURE
* HOUSE	R5000/MONTH	R2 400 000
* CAR	R2200/MONTH	R1 056 000
* INSURANCE	R2000/MONTH	R 960 000
* HOLIDAYS	R1000/MONTH	R 480 000
* EDUCATION	R2000/MONTH	R 960 000
* CLOTHES	R 200/MONTH	R 96 000
* ENTERTAINMENT	R 200/MONTH	R 96 000
* FOOD/GROCERY	R1500/MONTH	R 720 000

TOTAL EXPENDITURE   R6 768 000

SHORTFALL   **R1 968 000**

Now, even if you differ with some of the calculations, the bottom line is that life as a corporate employee is one long financial struggle. And you know what's really sad, many people who are corporate employees have the talent and energy to create their own work environment. And this carries far greater rewards, both personal and financial.

What often happens is that people become addicted to the small corporate perks like large offices, secretaries, parking next to the lift, and titles. But these perks assume an importance totally out of proportion to their worth.

The Alternative to Corporate Slavery

Let's take the example of a South African who has successfully run a well known franchise. In under 15 years, a typical operator would achieve what a corporate employee would achieve in 40 years. And, on top of that, the operator would still have an asset worth around

R2 million to sell at the end of it. The corporate employee, on the other hand, would end up with a nice gold watch.

In this book, we will give you all the options. We'll help you start your own business from scratch or we'll help you identify the right franchise for your needs. So if you are still a corporate employee right now, or if you're an ex corporate employee in the market for a future, welcome to an outstanding rest of your life!

The life of Mike and Eric

Both of us started life in large corporations. Both of us have been through the agony and ecstasy of failure and success. We know what it's like to experience frustration, fear, anxiety, depression, panic and anger. But we also know what it's like to experience joy, fulfillment, security, self-actualization and ultimate excitement.

That's why we're writing this book. We've been to the brink and back. We're two ordinary guys who've made a success by believing in ourselves, persevering, being honest and grabbing the opportunities with both hands as they flew by.

We're not going to lie to you by telling you that it's easy. It's not. But then nothing that's worth anything is easy. What we are going to tell you is that anyone can succeed if you implement the fundamental principles and strategies outlined in this book. But you need to implement these principles with passion and discipline. In fact, ultimately, passion and discipline are what this book is all about.

Mike's Story

I started my business career as a product manager at Colgate Palmolive learning how to sell soap and toothpaste. Then I moved to an advertising agency called Grey Phillips. That was seventeen years ago and that's where I met Eric Parker for the first time. He was working for a company selling pool cleaners and he became my client. We've stayed in contact over the years and now we are producing this book together. If there's one thing I've learnt, it's this: When you meet people of quality, keep the relationship alive. Quality relationships with quality people always pay out big time.

I spent five years at Grey Phillips before emigrating to Canada in 1987. There I joined another global advertising agency called

Ogilvy & Mather. Like many other South Africans who emigrate, I excelled in my job. Within eighteen months, I was promoted to a director responsible for almost R100 million rands worth of business.

Then, two years later, I plunged into deep, dark depression. What really caused the depression, I'll never know. But what contributed towards it was a series of bad financial and career decisions that robbed me of my confidence. And once your confidence goes, everything else follows. Nothing could help me out of my miserable state, not therapy, not drugs, not anything.

Eventually, at the end of 1991, I returned to South Africa - beaten, almost bankrupt and still in a state of mental breakdown. In February 1992, I was referred to a psychiatrist who prescribed electroconvulsive therapy as the cure for my mental disease. I was scared, but you know what? When you're at rock bottom, you can't fall any further. So I agreed to the treatment. I thought there was very little damage that could be done to a mind that was already almost damaged beyond repair.

Well, I had the shock treatment. And I recovered my mind, my motivation and my personal power in just one week. As quickly as my depression came, it disappeared. And since February 1992, I have never experienced depression again and I never will. I'm not saying I don't get the blues. That's normal. What I'm saying is that I've learnt to manage my moods - one of the most important skills an entrepreneur can have (We'll discuss mood management later in this book).

On 1 January 1993, I started my own business called Touch The Sky, The Imagination Company. My mission from the very beginning was to excite and motivate people. I was lucky enough to meet Reg Lascaris, the legendary co-founder of the Hunt Lascaris Advertising Agency. We wrote a book together just before the 1994 elections called Revelling In The Wild, Business Lessons Out Of Africa. We followed up that book with another one called Fire & Water, The Power of Passion, The Force of Flow. In between, I wrote my autobiography, Lost & Found. All three books became massive bestsellers. My career as a motivator, personal developer and trainer thrived. I've hosted my own programmes on radio and TV. At the end of 1998, I published another bestseller - Mampodi!! 100 Mindsparks to light up your head, heart, body and soul.

Looking back, it seems unbelievable that so much has been achieved since my recovery from depression in 1992. But that's what so many entrepreneurs have said to me. When they look back on what they have achieved, they are amazed. It's like a huge force greater than themselves has helped them succeed against all odds.

I live everyday in the light and power of that force. It lights my way in the darkness and the unknown. It's the force that comes from truly believing in yourself, what you do and what you give to others. The moment you commit yourself to your mission, you too will experience the force.

Why I wrote this book with Eric

Over the past seven years, I have specialized in the study of personal excellence. I have researched "The Right Stuff" and how we can all attain it. I have become the nation's leading authority on personal effectiveness, achievement and confidence. In the course of my journey, I have built a highly successful business, but I am not an authority on starting and managing a business. I can give you everything you need to stay focused, motivated and connected to others. But you need a master to teach you how to select, start and manage your own business for maximum results. That's why I chose Eric Parker. Eric Parker is one of South Africa's leading authorities on small business, marketing and franchising. He is also a straightshooter who operates out of total personal integrity.

If I am responsible for most of the passion in the book, Eric is responsible for most of the discipline. I'm the guy who revs you up and Eric is the guy who keeps you firmly on the road to success.

This is what I will give you in this book:

I want to share with you everything I've learnt since I started my own business on 1 January 1993. I will focus on how you can enter and stay in The Zone - that place where you reach your maximum potential and where you perform at the peak of your ability. I will show you how to achieve your personal greatness and help others do exactly the same. Specifically, we'll explore these vital ten areas of successful entrepreneurs:

- How to set a powerful purpose; How to gain total commitment; Learn the art of visualization; Set big but achievable goals.

- How to learn the Language of Success; Use empowering thinking; Master your emotions and those of others

- How to achieve and sustain massive confidence; How to identify and express your values and those of your business; Using non-verbal communication Skills; Acquiring BMT - Big Match Temperament.

- How to achieve absolute consistency in everyday performance; Adopting a zero excuses approach to life; Guaranteeing results through the mental preparation of champions.

- How to develop resilience and master the art of mistake recovery; How to make mistakes work for you; Overcoming failure; The importance of leisure and re-creation.

- How to develop creativity and innovation; How to think laterally and generate options.

- How to maximize human potential - both yours and the people around you; The vital leadership skills; The power of curiousity; Staying young; Becoming a mentor.

- How to love the game even when it turns against you; Staying enthusiastic; How to rally the people around you, especially in tough times; How to protect yourself from other people's criticisms and insults.

- How to develop and use the power of self-awareness; The results that come from consciously thinking about your words and deeds; How to ask the right questions all the time.

- How to develop the persistence of the Cheetah; Learn to love setbacks; Stay focused when you're tired; Trying new things all the time.

Eric's story

I came from a humble but happy family living in Malvern, Johannesburg. My dad was a carpenter by trade and he was crazy about golf and boxing, which is why he made me fight. I was actually quite a timid guy but getting a bloody nose was not my idea of fun so I learnt to fight back. This was a lesson that has held me in good stead my whole life.

I went to Jeppe Boy's High and in STD 9, my class set a record - the whole class failed. Eventually, though, I managed to pass matric. I wanted to study marketing but my dad was against it because he didn't believe it was a "solid" profession. I studied metallurgy instead. I went to work for Haggie Rand, a major steel wire rope company. In my spare time, I studied marketing and passed the three-year diploma in marketing management through the IMM. The moment I discovered marketing, I knew I had found my niche. I loved it. It was a three year programme and I did well.

After Haggie Rand, I went to another large industrial company, Stewarts&Lloyds. But I really wanted to get into marketing somehow. Then I saw an ad for a Group Product Manager at Carlton Paper. I really wanted the job but I had no experience. I met a man called Keith Partridge who was the marketing director at the time. Although I had no experience, Keith took a gamble and hired me. I stayed there for seven years, rising to marketing manager.

Then I joined Permkleen Pool, the company that manufactured and marketed Kreepy Krauly, as Managing Director. At the time, it was a relatively small, entrepreneurial company. And that's where I learnt how to be streetwise. I helped build Kreepy Krauly into a very successful business.

After five years, I left to join Kentucky Fried Chicken as Marketing Director. I stayed there for six years. I loved the business. I learnt an enormous amount about franchising and I helped the company and the franchisees make lots of money.

After Kentucky Fried Chicken, I joined a company that identified great businesses, bought them, developed them and then sold or listed them on the Stock Exchange. It was while I was at this company that I was introduced to Robby Brozin, the guy who started up Nando's. Robbie knew about my experience with Kentucky Fried Chicken and invited me to join Nando's as a co-founder. We really got Nando's going in 1987. In the seven years that I was with Nando's, I helped build the business from one store in Savoy, Johannesburg, to over eighty stores nationwide.

I left Nando's to start up a Franchise Consultancy with Bendeta Gordon, a Chartered Accountant. I focused on the marketing aspects of Franchising and she provided the Financial expertise. The Consultancy was phenomenally successful. We became known as the leader in Franchising expertise in South Africa. We did work for such clients as MTN, Standard Bank and BP. Bendeta then decided to go her own way and I was bought out by Deloitte&Touche. I am now Director of Franchising at Deloitte & Touche. I was also the Chairman of the Franchise Association of South Africa from 1992 to 1995 as well as being Franchise Personality of the Year in 1995.

Why I wrote this book with Mike Lipkin

I wrote this book with Mike because he gets people excited. He also has the ability to mobilise their energy to make things happen. On the other hand, I have over 30 years marketing experience. I am a recognised authority on Franchising and business start-ups, but sometimes I get frustrated because of the prevailing attitudes in South Africa.

You know why? Because in our schools, universities and the private sector in general, there is still the belief that it's better to work for a boss than for yourself. I still see students obsessed with getting their CV's to large companies so they can be hired as an employee. I meet people who have been laid off, downsized or fired, immediately start the search for another job - only to be demoralized and frustrated. Together with Mike, I want to change the mindsets of South Africans from employee to entrepreneur.

What I will give you in this book:

I want to use my three decades of experience in marketing and franchising to make it easy for you to identify, start and manage your own business. I want to help free you from corporate bondage. I want to help you experience the rush of being your own boss. I want to help you make the most of your life, because, after all, we only move through this world once.

And you know what, it's not difficult. In many ways, it's much harder to work for a boss. What's more, working for large companies is not a guarantee of security anymore. Even government has become a risky place to work. In fact, the only true source of security is your own business.

Specifically, I will take you through the following seven steps to starting and managing your own successful business:

1. Starting and running your business: A roll-up-your-sleeves, hands-on approach
2. Making a Plan: how to construct a workable business plan
3. How to make your business sexy: designing and executing a great marketing program.
4. Raising cash: Cash Generators vs Cash Absorbers
5. Controlling your cash flow because cash flow is king
6. Managing the most important asset you'll ever have: your people
7. Looking after your customers in such a way that they stay with you for life - without them, you don't have a life.

Then, in the final section of this book, I will give you a selection of quality Franchise opportunities that you can explore.

"Help me help you, help me help you, help me help you"
Jerry Maguire

This book is a partnership between you and us. We want you to help us help you achieve your dream. This book is designed to help you design your game plan for success. In every section, we'll ask you questions that must be answered there and then. Please do not move on to the next section saying to yourself that you'll do it later. We promise you that you won't. Whatever you don't do immediately, you don't do!! We're demonstrating our commitment to you by writing this book. Please demonstrate your commitment to yourself by following through on the questions we ask you.

We don't expect you to have all the answers immediately. But you know what? Once you ask your brain a great question, it begins to find the answer. Questions are like signposts that guide the brain to think in a certain direction. Ask and eventually you will receive.

What's more, by asking new questions, you begin to develop your mental muscle. You begin to use areas of your brain that may be lying dormant. It's like going to gym. At first, the exercise seems awkward and uncomfortable. Your muscles get stiff, you run out of breath easily. But then after a while, your body becomes fitter and fitter; you can do more and more. And before you know it, your body starts to show the benefits of your endeavours. It's the same with your brain. You've got all that reserve mental energy that's just waiting to be used. Use it now!

A final promise before you get going:

We promise that everything we tell you in this book works. Every action we tell you to take has been tested in the Eric Parker and Mike Lipkin School of Life. We are not two academics sitting in some ivory tower. We are two entrepreneurs who have climbed rock by rock to the top of the Business Mountain. We have fallen. We have the scars. We have sweated and bled with the best of them.

We're here as your emotional and practical mentors. This book is our way of guiding you through the challenging, sometimes scary journey to becoming a successful entrepreneur.

May the Force be with you!

Part One:

Getting Into The High-Performance Zone:

That place where you perform at the peak of your ability; where you are unstoppable; where your thoughts and actions merge to deliver personal greatness

Getting into The High-Performance Zone

Have you ever watched Hugh Masekela play the trumpet? Have you ever watched Benni McCarthy score a goal? Have you ever watched Joost van der Westhuizen tear open the opposition's defense for a try? Have you ever watched Sharon Stone act? Has a waiter in a restaurant who never lost his cool or his sense of humour ever served you? Have you ever seen anyone do anything superbly well?

Have you noticed how the professionals and the artists make it look so easy? They seem to perform complex and difficult tasks without even thinking. It's like they are doing it instinctively and naturally. Well, they are. They're in The Zone - that place where they perform at the peak of their ability; where they are unstoppable; where their actions and thoughts join to deliver personal greatness.

All acts of excellence are performed by people in The Zone. It doesn't matter whether that act of excellence is a shop owner selling to his customers, a computer programmer designing a powerful software package or a chef preparing a great meal. The common denominator of excellence is total focus + preparation + application + passion + persistence. When we witness acts of excellence we are really witnessing the coming together of weeks, months, years of dedication. We are seeing the tip of the iceberg. We do not see all the pain and trauma that got the performer to that level.

As you read this book, are you noticing how easily it flows? Are you motivated to read the next page? Are you already feeling the excitement that comes with making your own dream happen? If you are, it's because both of us are in The Zone while we write this book. We are totally focused on making this book one of your most useful tools to help you start and manage your business successfully. We are passionate about the insight and secrets we are sharing with you. Both of us have already applied this knowledge in the marketplace. We know what works and what doesn't.

What you will not notice in the book is how long it took us to write it. You will not notice all the sweat, fatigue, setbacks, mistakes and upsets that we experienced while putting this book together. You see, it's because of all that effort and application that we stayed in The Zone. It's because of all the effort we put into the book that the book appears effortless.

And that's the first powerful secret of success. You must make it look easy. Your customers must feel relaxed and reassured because you radiate that sense of control and competence. Think about all the great moments, which you have experienced as a consumer of someone else's products or services. We guarantee you that the golden thread tying all the moments of excellence together is this visible lack of tension or anxiety in the delivery of the service or product.

But here's the ultimate truth: There is no easy walk into The Zone. You can't perform like a Champion without training like a Champion. You know, in Mike's seminars across the country, he asks delegates how many of them love to win. Almost everyone raises their hands. Then he asks delegates how many of them love to train so hard it hurts. Almost no one raises their hands. The bottom line is that you must be prepared to pay the price of success.

In our opinion, most failures in life are caused by three reasons:

1. **Lack of direction.** If you don't truly know where you're going, how can you really get there? As Stephen Covey says in his best-selling 7 Habits of Highly Effective People, begin with the end in mind. We will explore this issue in depth.

2. **Lack of preparation.** Just as you cannot build a building without a solid foundation, you cannot start a business without solid training, knowledge or commitment. Once again, we will cover this issue comprehensively.

3. **Lack of faith.** This may just be the biggest reason of all why people don't achieve their goals in life. They make minor failures total failures. They don't realize that the road to dreams is paved with setbacks. These minor failures and setbacks are really powerful lessons designed to strengthen you and your business.

There has never been a successful business anywhere on Planet Earth that has not stood the test of time by going through setbacks and failures. The magic ingredient that gets you through these tough times is Faith, the unshakeable conviction that you will get through the rough times and prevail over your problems, enemies, competitors and environment.

If you do not have this unshakeable conviction, stop reading this book now and give it to someone who does. Honestly, go inside yourself right now. Take a couple moments to think about whether you truly believe you have it within you to start and run a successful business. Deep down, are you one of the courageous few who are willing to put their life, their resources and their reputation on the line to achieve their dreams?

If you're still reading this book, it must mean that you're serious about making your dreams happen. So are we. So let's explore how to enter and stay in The Zone.

The Power of Purpose, Commitment & Visualization

"The purpose of life is a life of purpose!"

George Bernard Shaw.

The main thing is to keep the main thing the main thing. What's yours? Seriously, think for a moment why you were put on Planet Earth. Answer the following seven Purpose, Commitment & Visualization questions:

What is the one most important benefit you provide to other people?

_____

_____

What are you truly great at? Or what could you be truly great at?

_____

_____

What do you love doing the most?

_____

_____

What important things are you truly committed to doing?

_____

_____

What are the three biggest goals that you want to achieve in the next twelve months?

_____

_____

What is the biggest contribution that you want to make to your community over the next twelve months?

_____

_____

If your life over the next twelve months were a movie, What kind of ending to the movie do you see for yourself?

_____

_____

The Power of Purpose

In his book, Man's Search For Meaning, Viktor Frankl tells of his experiences in the Nazi Concentration Camps during the Second World War. He states that the reason why he survived while so many people around him perished is that he had a "Why" that empowered him to find the "How" of survival. Frankl's reason for survival was that he wanted the world to know what happened in the camp so that it never happened again. He knew that whatever happened, he would survive because his purpose was so important. Frankl stated that so many people perished because they had no powerful reason to go on living in those hellish conditions.

Now, thank God, you and we are not living in a concentration camp. And yet we meet so many people who are so miserable that they might as well may be. They don't have an empowering purpose to guide them. They put themselves first in every situation. They don't see their role as helping to improve the quality of life of the people around them.

Every person we have met who has sustained a high level of success over time, has had a purpose that continually guides him or her through their life and their business. A purpose is like a compass that always points to true north no matter where you may be. So what's your purpose?

What are you truly great at?

Once you think you know your purpose, ask yourself what you are truly great at. Or what you could be truly great at. For example, if your purpose is to empower people by writing books but you can't write then it is unlikely you will achieve your purpose. But, for example, if your purpose is to make people happy by feeding them great food and you are a great cook, then you're cooking with gas! *Your skills or potential skills must serve your purpose.*

What do you truly love doing?

We promise you that you will never be a great success at something you hate doing. Unless you do what you love, you'll never love what you do. So what do you truly love doing? And how could you turn what you are doing into a commercial success? So, by way of illustration, Mike loves talking and he has turned his passion into a commercial success through motivational speaking. Eric loves helping people become independent and that's what he now does for a living.

What are you truly committed to?

Commitment: Pledge or Promise. (Webster's Dictionary)

It's one thing to want to do something. It's a completely different thing to have to do something. If you just want to do something, you'll probably never do it. But if you totally commit to do something with all your heart and soul, you'll move mountains.

We were totally committed to writing this book. Despite the fact that we had to continue with our hectic business schedules, we finished this book on time because we made a pledge to ourselves and to each other. And once you make a pledge, there's no going back.

The greatest source of inner satisfaction and fulfillment is honouring the pledge you make to yourself and others. And the greatest source of pain and guilt is neglecting your pledges. Everyday, we meet people who promise one thing and do something else. These are people who are losing their personal power. They are losing respect for themselves. Their word is not their bond. It's just hot air. And remember, the moment you lose respect for yourself, others will begin to lose respect for you. And that's the beginning of the end.

Commitment is power. The person with the most commitment always wins. Do you know why? Because they simply cannot give up or give in. They persist until they succeed.

But here's a little warning: Do not commit to actions or outcomes that may have negative consequences for others. Do not commit to things that will only benefit you. Do not commit to anything that you think may be immoral or unsustainable. Rather, commit to those things that will bless others along the way. Commit to those things that will empower others to achieve their goals. Do you know why? Because we are all interdependent. A person is a person because of other people.

Here's a powerful question for you to think about as you focus on starting or taking your business to the next level: How will your success lead to the happiness, well being and success of others? If the answer to that question is clear, your success will be certain.

What are the three biggest goals that you want to achieve in the next twelve months?

We believe a big goal is really a dream with a deadline. If you are going to achieve your goals, you must know what they are. You must be able to describe it and to measure it. It must be specific. It must be inspirational to you and to the people you need to help you achieve it. It must be big enough to stretch you but small enough to be achievable.

Very few people take the time to identify their three biggest goals in any twelve-month period. They are more concerned with getting through the day than getting the kind of life they truly desire. You know why? Because most people are reactive. They wait for life to direct them and then they try and respond. That's why many people are always in crisis mode. They bounce from one problem to the next like a pinball.

But you are proactive. We know that because otherwise you would not have invested in this book and you would not have read this far. You take the time to think ahead; to anticipate; to design the outcomes you truly want. So set your 12 months goals now. This book will help give you the strategy to realize them.

If your life over the next twelve months were a movie, What kind of ending to the movie do you see for yourself?

Everything in life is created twice. First in your own mind and then in reality. So what have you already seen on the big screen inside your head? What is the happy ending to your twelve-month movie?

One of the most powerful psychological discoveries of the 20th century is that *your mind cannot tell the difference between what really happens to you and what you imagine is happening to you.* That's why those people who have learnt to use the power of visualization radiate such certainty and confidence. In their own minds, they have already seen themselves as being successful. Then they go out and persuade others to help them in their quest.

All Champion athletes see themselves winning the contest before they actually participate in the contest. First they win in their mind, and then they win in reality. Their imagination muscles strengthen their physical muscles. They have learnt so see into the future - their desired future.

Are you a Champion? It doesn't matter what business you want to start, if you can truly see yourself being successful, you'll be successful. But you must be able to see a picture that is sharply defined. You must be able to describe the picture in such a way that anyone around you can see it almost as clearly as you. Come on, try it now. Go describe your movie ending to a person who you can trust. Are you fluent? Are you excited? Are you getting the other person excited? Do you know exactly what you want to happen? Can you make it brighter, clearer, bigger? What does it sound like? What does it smell like? What does it feel like? Make it so real to yourself that you are convinced you are already there. If you have even a shred of doubt that it will not happen, it will not happen!

Mike's answers to the 7 Purpose, Commitment and Visualization questions

Mike's purpose and number one benefit to others is "To Excite People Into Action". Everything that Mike does, from his motivational talks to his audiotapes to his books, is meant to Excite People Into Action. When Mike is approached with a business opportunity or when he is investigating an opportunity, he only asks himself one question, "Will this help me excite people into action?" As a result of Mike's purpose, he remains focused, committed and persistent.

Mike believes that he is truly great at speaking and writing and that he was meant to use these skills to empower others. More than anything else, Mike loves sharing knowledge with people and getting them excited.

He is committed to bringing South Africans the most powerful motivational and success technology from all over the world. He wants to help thousands South Africans realize their potential and live the life of their dreams. His three biggest goals over the next twelve months are:

1. To ensure this book sells over 30,000 copies
2. Together with Eric Parker, to help 10,000 South Africans launch their own businesses through this book, live seminars and audio/videotapes.
3. To achieve the highest level of mental, spiritual and physical fitness

so that he can sustain the pace required to make the first two goals happen. He will know he has achieved this when he weighs 80 kilograms, can run 10 kilometres in 50 minutes, has a resting pulse rate of 50 beats per minute, feels a strong sense of inner quietness and serenity, and is continually creative and motivated.

The biggest contribution that Mike wants to make to the country in the next twelve months is to help over 50,000 South Africans get the confidence and the tools to make their lives successful.

If the next twelve months of Mike's life were a movie, the ending he would see for himself is to be the person who has made a difference in almost 100,000 people's lives. Mike sees himself as South Africa's Number One motivator who has achieved his own personal goals by helping so many other South Africans achieve theirs. He sees himself as someone who crosses all cultural, class and colour lines to connect and impact people positively. He sees their smiles. He feels their handshakes of love and gratitude. He hears their applause and shouts of joy. He smells the sweet smell of success - both theirs and his.

Eric's answers to the 7 Purpose, Commitment and Visualization questions

Eric's purpose and number one benefit to others is "Making People Independent through Knowledge and Self-Belief". Everything Eric is doing right now is aimed at giving people an alternative to a no-win, dead-end corporate career. Eric's total focus is on empowering people to help themselves. This book is another way for him to implement his purpose.

Eric believes that his key strengths are creative thinking and the ability to spot trends and make predictions for the future. Five years ago, Eric was already predicting the decline of major corporations as sources of employment. That's why he specialised in franchising and small business.

Eric loves meeting new people and taking on new challenges. He loves exploring new territories and guiding others through the unknown. In fact, he sees himself as a business guide and coach in turbulent times.

Eric is totally committed to creating more employment in South Africa through small business. On a conceptual level, he is totally

committed to shattering the mindset of being a job seeker to being a job creator. Eric's three biggest goals over the next twelve months are:
1. Increase Franchising from 9% to 14% of all retail sales.
2. Establish Deloitte & Touche Franchising Consultancy as the undisputed leader in Franchising in South Africa.
3. To instill a powerful entrepreneurial spirit into his children:
    - Firstly, his daughter, Linda Oerder, who has successfully started her own physio practice at the Sandton Clinic
    - Secondly, his sons - Barry and Greg - who, in partnership with the Howie family, are developing the Seattle Coffee franchise in South Africa.

The biggest contribution that Eric wants to make to his community over the next 12 months is to help people establish their self-respect and financial independence without relying on large companies. Specifically, Eric wants to help those people who have been retrenched get back on their feet with enthusiasm and pride.

If the next twelve months of Eric's life were a movie, he would see himself as the father of entrepreneurship in South Africa. Eric knows it is a big personal vision, but it's a massively exciting vision. Eric wants to be the guy who showed thousands of South Africans that there is another way - the self directed and self-managed way.

"If you build it, they will come"
Kevin Costner

Okay, by now you should be fully aware of the power of purpose, commitment and visualization. You should also have attempted to define your purpose, commitment and visualization. But if your image of the future isn't razor sharp for you yet, don't worry. You've ignited the process. You've got your motor running. To truly get into The Zone, though, you have to focus on the 7 Questions of Purpose, Commitment and Visualization everyday until you have an "AHA EXPERIENCE". What's an "AHA EXPERIENCE"? It's when one day, at a time when you may least expect it, the answers come to you. And they will come to you if you truly believe they will come to you. We know. We talk from our own experience.

The Thoughts and Language of Success:

How to use empowered thinking to master your emotions and those of others

"As a man thinks, so he becomes"
James Allen

Have you ever noticed how bad things happen to you when you are in a bad mood? Have you noticed how you repulse and offend people when you are negative? Have you noticed how many things you do and say that you later regret when you are feeling down? Have you noticed how little energy you have when you are depressed? Have you noticed how few ideas you have when you are focused on why the world is a horrible place to be? Finally, have you noticed how you lose all your personal power when you are out of emotional control?

On the other hand, have you noticed how many great things happen to you when you are excited? Have you noticed how other people enjoy being around you? Have you noticed how inspired you are when you are exhilarated? Have you noticed how much energy you have? Have you noticed how many great ideas start flowing through you? Most importantly, have you noticed that when you are in a great mood, you feel like you can do anything? You feel like you are Superman, Batman and Einstein all rolled into one.

Well, what do you think puts you in a bad mood or a great mood? Do you think it's your environment? Do you think it's other people? Do you think it's the results you've achieved? Do you think it's your genes? Are you the kind of person who is in a great mood when things are going well and in a bad mood when things go badly? Do things outside your control dictate your mood swings?

Or are you the kind of person who can control their emotions? Are you the kind of person who stays calm when others panic? Are you the kind of person who inspires others in tough times? Are you at your best when things are at their worst? Do you control your moods irrespective of what's going on around you? Do you consistently nurture the people around you with your words and actions?

Thought is the highest human energy.
Whatever we think, that's what we attract to us

If there is one unchallengeable truth that we can share with you in this book, it's this: If you cannot control your thoughts, you can never succeed. If you get upset easily, you can never succeed. If you are easily offended, insulted or disappointed, you can never succeed. If you let your environment control your emotions, you can never succeed.

Successful entrepreneurs are human generators of their own energy and optimism. They have the powerful ability to detect the opportunity in the midst of chaos and uncertainty. They insulate themselves against the negativity of others. In fact, where others find reasons to despair, they find reasons to celebrate. They know that it is not what happens to them that is important, it's the meaning they attach to what happens to them. While others find disempowering meaning in problems or crises, they always look for the empowering lesson.

Look at this book for example. If South Africa were not going through massive transition, if South Africans were not experiencing crises on many levels, if there was not so much downsizing or business failures, there would be no reason to write this book. We saw the problem: Massive numbers of people either wanting or having to start their own businesses but not knowing how. We saw the solution: Produce the first book that effectively combines motivation and inspiration with practical business guidance.

Many people ask Mike why he doesn't return to Canada because he has Canadian citizenship. Mike responds by saying that in Canada, there's no role for him. Things are so calm and stable there that Mike's input is probably not needed. In South Africa, however, Mike believes he can make a massive difference. The very reasons why he is so excited about this country are the reasons that make many people depressed.

What effect do you have on others?
What effect do you have on yourself?

Have you ever noticed how someone can walk into a room and you can immediately feel whether their energy is positive or negative? Have you also noticed how you can walk into a store or a restaurant and immediately sense whether the people are turned on or turned off?

The real reason why you and we associate with certain people or businesses is how they make us feel. Ultimately, those people and businesses that make us feel great will succeed and those who don't will fail. The energy that you radiate will either make you or break you. That's why there are so many restaurants and stores that look beautiful but fail. And that's why there are so many clever people who fail as well. Their strategy is right, their knowledge is right, but their energy is wrong.

The most powerful magnet for success is positive energy. Especially in hard times, people crave people who are positive. Be that kind of person by learning to control your thoughts, because your thoughts control your emotions. And your emotions control your physical health. For example, right now please think deeply about the following things:

- The person who irritates you the most in your life
- The last time you had an accident on the road.
- The last fight you had with your spouse or loved one.
- The last time you read about a crime
- The last time you felt you were treated unfairly
- The last big disappointment you had
- The last time you were rejected or hurt
- The thing that you are most worried about right now

Notice what happens when you focus on negative things: Your heart starts to beat faster; your body becomes tense; you feel a tightness in your stomach; you start to take shorter breaths; you grind your teeth; you feel a sense of rage; you feel helpless; you feel immobilised; you feel slightly numb; you break into a cold sweat.

In other words, when you focus on negative things, you experience negative physical symptoms. In fact, you experience physical disease. Now please focus on the following positive things:

- The three people who you love most in your life
- The happiest moment of your life
- The one thing that you are most grateful for in your life
- One reason why you should be excited right now
- The first time you ever made love
- The most successful day of your life
- A time when someone really helped you
- The funniest movie you've ever seen

Now notice what happens when you think about positive things: You breathe deeply; you smile; you relax; you feel excited; you nod your head up and down confirming how good life can be; you feel the adrenaline start to flow through your body; you feel strong; you want to move around.

In other words, your positive thoughts have created a positive physical state. So here's the secret of mentally tough people: They never lose focus on the positive things in their lives. They never allow their current environment or situation to hijack their mental and physical well being. They are bigger than any obstacle that confronts them.

We are not saying that you shouldn't feel negative emotions such as anger, fear, frustration or disappointment. That's only human. What we're saying is that you can't allow these emotions to own you. The person who can get through these emotions fastest is the person who will ultimately win.

As an entrepreneur, there's one thing you can be certain of: There will be days when you feel like giving up; there will be moments when you feel like you can't go on; there will be times when you will feel massively frustrated; There will be days when the whole world seems to have turned against you. That's when your commitment will be put to the test. That's when your ability to control your thoughts and emotions will be tried. That's when you will show your true strength or that's when you will crumble.

So right now, start building your inventory of positive thoughts. Start gathering all the great things in your life and write them down. Keep these thoughts and things close to you at all times. Focus on them when you need the power to get through dark times.

And never lose sight of your purpose, commitment and goals. Successful entrepreneurs survive and thrive because they constantly remind themselves why they are doing what they are doing.

Recently, Mike visited Robbin Island where an ex-political prisoner guided him through the prison. Mike asked the prisoner how he survived eight years of abuse and hardship in prison. The guide replied by saying that there were three things that helped him survive: firstly, he never doubted that his cause was right and his captors were wrong; secondly, he accepted his surroundings as his reality but he didn't allow them to break his spirit; and thirdly, he learnt to go inside himself and remind himself of all the reasons why he was grateful to be alive. Makes you think, doesn't it?

The Language of Transformation:
Are you on a permanent mental diet?

Look at your watch. For the next 30 seconds, please sit still and watch the second hand move. Do it now. Do not read on until you have done this exercise.

Welcome back. What did you hear while you watched your watch? You probably heard some sounds outside of yourself. But what did you hear coming from inside your head? In other words, what thoughts were you listening to? Did you say, this is a dumb exercise? Or did you say, I wonder why I'm being asked to do this? Or did your mind wander? Did you think about other things in your life right now?

What's our point? We are continually thinking. And what is thinking but speaking to ourselves? And the words we say to ourselves determine our attitude; our mood; our happiness and ultimately, our success or failure. So here's one of the most important points of the entire book:

You cannot control what's going outside your head, but you are the absolute boss of your inner reality.

People who sustain a high level of success have the ability to talk to themselves and to other people in a consistently empowering way. They stand guard at the door of their mind. They ensure that the words they say to themselves and others are encouragements not demotivators. Even when they feel the need to use disempowering words to communicate with others, they discipline themselves not to vent their negative emotions on the people around them. Do you?

You see, many of us have got into the habit of speaking negatively. We have got used to moaning and groaning. And we do it without even being aware of it. Well, from today, make a conscious decision to talk in Power Words - both to yourself and to others.

Power Words are words designed to give you and the people around you personal power. Here are some examples:

Negative Words	_Power Words_
I can't	I will
If only	No regrets, only tomorrows
They'll never accept that	I'll convince them
I hate that person	I understand that person
Big Problem	Exciting Challenge
It's too much for me	Now, I get to stretch myself
That person bugs me	that person increases my tolerance levels
It's hopeless	There's always a way
It will never work	I'll find a way or make a way
You can't trust anyone	People are dependable but practice vigilance
I hope I can do it	I know I can do it
I should	I must
Tomorrow	Right now
Maybe	Definitely
I'm worried	I anticipate and I will act
It's not my fault	Here's how we can fix it
It's not my problem	We're all in it together
What if we fail?	What must we do to ensure success?
It was a bad experience	It was a great lesson
I'm at the end of my rope	I'm about to climb to the next level.
I don't know what to do	I'm on the verge of a breakthrough
It's just too much effort	I'll do whatever it takes

So what are your Power Words? Please do this exercise now:
Think of the most common negative words and phrases you usually use. Write them down, one underneath each other. Then replace them with a Power Word. And commit to using this Power Word constantly. And by the way, you may not even be aware of the negative words that you use, so ask the people around you to help you in this process.

Deposit into the "Feel Good" account

If you really want to turbo-boost your spirit and the spirit of the people around you, commit to paying at least ten compliments a day to others and to yourself. Catch other people doing things right and catch yourself doing things right.

Everytime you pay someone a compliment (including yourself), you make a deposit in the "Feel Good" account. You feel good about yourself and others feel good about you. And really, isn't that what life is all about? All of us do what we do so that we can feel good. So put this book down now and go pay three compliments as follows:

1. Pay someone a compliment face to face
2. Pay someone a compliment over the phone
3. Pay yourself a compliment

A Warning: When we ask you to pay someone a compliment, we ask you to do it with absolute sincerity. Don't be false. And don't be shallow. Pay people compliments about things that are important to them. Even if it feels awkward at first, you'll soon get used to it.

The Magic Ingredient of Achievement: Massive, Unshakeable Confidence

'I'm the greatest!"
Mohammed Ali

After studying highly successful entrepreneurs for almost twenty years, we believe that their most powerful personal resource is their massive, unshakeable, confidence.

And by confidence, we don't mean arrogance. In fact, arrogance is a guarantee of failure.

Arrogance is defined by the dictionary as: making claims that cannot be supported; pretensions to superiority; insolently proud.

Confidence is defined as: Having full trust; belief in the reliability of a person; assurance or boldness; sure of oneself; having no uncertainty about one's own abilities.

Without massive, unshakeable confidence, nothing else happens. Confidence is the ability to look failure in the eye and see right through it. Confidence is the power to see beyond temporary problems to the ultimate solutions. Confidence is the belief in your own ability even when everything around you may be turning against you. Confidence means never, ever putting yourself down or feeling sorry for yourself. Confidence is the glue that holds you together in tough times. Do you have it?

Confidence does not mean that you never doubt yourself or that you never feel nervous. Confidence doesn't mean that you're always ready to take on any challenge. And it also doesn't mean that you always know exactly what you want.

Confidence is really the belief that you have what it takes to succeed. It is an acceptance of your responsibility to your creator to do the great things that He designed you to do. Confidence is the power that comes from recognising your higher power. It is the knowledge that you are bigger than any problem life can throw at you.

Your Personal Confidence Test

Here is a simple twelve point test to determine your confidence levels. For each question, rate yourself on a scale of 1-10. Think about each question and answer it with total honesty (no-one will see the results but you):

1. Are you proud of yourself? _____
2. If you don't have the skills you need, can you learn them fast? _____
3. Do you know exactly what you want and how you're going to get it? _____
4. Do you make decisions quickly? _____
5. When you talk, do people listen to you? _____
6. Do you care deeply about others? _____
7. When you think of change, are you excited? _____
8. Do you like talking in front of a group of people? _____
9. Is your life an exhilarating adventure? _____
10. When others doubt you, do you stay self-assured? _____
11. In tough times, are you optimistic? _____
12. Are you the kind of person who influences others? _____

TOTAL _____

If you scored 105-120, you are supremely confident. You're a confidence champion. You are ready to take on any challenge. If you haven't taken the leap into the unknown, do it now.

If you scored 90-104, you are very confident. You're a confidence contender. You are well equipped to go where you haven't been before. By concentrating on the key areas for developing your confidence even more, you will become unstoppable.

If you scored 72-89, you are reasonably confident. You have your moments. But you still have major work to do before you are ready to put yourself and your future on the line. Concentrate on the key areas where you need to augment your confidence. Study this book. Take the test again in a month.

If you scored less than 72, your confidence levels need boosting. Fear may have a grip on your mind and your heart. You may have a habit of thinking and acting that is disempowering you. Go within. Identify the source of your fear. Come to terms with it. Manage it. Master it. Study this book. Take the test again in three months.

Hug your fear

At the beginning of this book, we said that courage isn't the absence of fear, it's the determination to act despite your fear.

If you want massive confidence, we're now going to tell you that you have to hug your fear. Learn to celebrate your fear. Accept it. Welcome it. Treat it like a trusted friend. You know why? Because you would not be human if you didn't feel fear any time you took a big risk or began something you didn't know you could do.

We still feel fear. Our fear keeps us sharp. It keeps us from becoming complacent or comfortable. Our fear also stimulates us to perform better and better. In fact, fear has become one of our biggest allies in our quest to take ownership of our markets.

And that's the difference between people who stay successful and those who don't: The best of the breed have learnt to use their fear as a source of competitive advantage; the rest have succumbed to their fear as a source of uncertainty and self-doubt. What's your relationship with your fear?

We believe that fear is really just a signal from your brain that you need to be alert, prepared and ready to adapt to anything, anytime, anywhere.

The bottom line is that fear, like heat, is a human necessity. Use it well, and you achieve well being. Misuse it, and you get burnt. From now on, when you feel fear, ask yourself only two questions:

1. *Is this fear justified or is it just my imagination?*
2. *How do I use this fear to move forward?*

Love the pressure: Build your BMT

You know when massive confidence really gets results? In the big pressure moments. How many people do you know who "choke" under pressure? They're fine as long as things are going well. But when the chocolate hits the fan, they come undone.

Know this truth: It's in the high-pressure moments that you define yourself. That's when you demonstrate your true character. That's when you reach for the stars or grovel in the gutter. That's why we are so grateful for the pressure. It's our opportunity to show what we're really made of. It's our chance to strengthen our mental muscle so that we can take even more pressure in the next round. We use the pressure to develop BMT - Big Match Temperament.

As an independent businessperson, we can promise you that you will be under continual pressure. Even when your business is flying, you'll be under pressure to do even better. Unless you love it, it will crush you.

Know thyself: your values are your true source of confidence

Confidence is really a form of personal certainty. Confidence is the opposite of doubt and confusion. So, the only real way you can have total confidence is to know what you really want in life. In other words, you have to know what the most important things in your life are - your values.

In our seminars around the country, less than 1% of people can tell us what their values are, ranked in order of priority. And we say: Unless you know what you truly want, how can you get it? If you aren't aware of your deepest needs, how can they be satisfied? And how can you be confident?

So please do this exercise with us right now: rank your eight top values in order of priority and think deeply about why you're doing it. If you've never done this before, here's a simple way to do it. Write down all the things that are important to you in life. Do not prioritise. Come on, think of everything that you either want or need deeply. Then review your list and order them in importance from 1-8. It ain't easy, is it? But you know what, just by doing this exercise, you're clearing your mind. You're getting to the core of who and what you are. And once you're there, your confidence will soar because it's coming from the centre of you.

Mike's top 8 values are:	Eric's top 8 values are:
Courage	Enthusiasm/passion
Growth	Honesty
Independence	Love
Contribution	Contribution
Love	Independence
Adventure	Being down to earth
Passion	Courage
Making a difference	Caring about others

And by the way, we didn't feature the most important value of all, Integrity, because that is a given. Without integrity, nothing else can sustain itself.

We promise you that if you identify your true values, prioritise them correctly and live by them, you will experience a power and serenity that are the roots of massive confidence.

The Hollywood Principle: Become a great actor; Become the roles you have to play

Think about the best communicators you know. What is the common denominator among all of them? It's more than just the words they use, right? It's the way they communicate. It's their posture; their tone of voice; the way they look at you; their smile; their sincerity; their caring; their laughter; and their energy.

Most communication is non-verbal. By that we mean, it is far more than just the actual words which are spoken. When you are with someone, subconsciously you are evaluating everything about them: whether you like them; whether they know what they're talking about; whether they are enjoying themselves being with you; whether you are enjoying yourself being with them; whether you can trust them; whether they can help you or not; whether they are the kind of person with whom you would like to build a relationship; whether they share your values; whether they are competent and confident. And when you are with others, they are doing exactly the same with you.

So here's a secret of highly successful people: *They adapt to different people and situations by playing whatever role they need to play in the circumstances. They do not expect others to adapt to them.*

One of the main differences between those who succeed and those who don't is that the Successes do things the Failures don't want to do or don't feel like doing. We promise you that people like being with people who are like them or how they would like to be. So if you really want to influence others and get them to want to buy from you, be an actor. Play the role that will win you their Academy Award. Put your own attitudes and habits aside and assume theirs. You'll see how quickly you get results.

Now, we aren't saying "be false". We aren't saying "Don't be yourself". We're saying, "Play the role you want to receive." Project yourself into your desired scenario and act as though you are already there. Please do this exercise now:

Think of three people who you need to influence. Think of the three results that you want from each person. Think about what kind of person each of those three people are. Think about what they like most. Now think about what role you need to play to connect with each one of those people and get the results you want. Visualize yourself getting the result. See it clearly. Play the roles you need to play. Enjoy your success.

Burn Your Excuses:

The Core Quality of Champion Entrepreneurs is Absolute, Relentless, Unyielding Consistency

"Anyone can have an excellent game.
Only the best have game excellence!"
Anthony Robbins

Think about one of the biggest reasons why people don't succeed. We promise you it's their inability to sustain a consistent level of personal excellence. Time and time again, we meet people who have made it and lost it. They get to the top then they tumble down again.

Think about those people whom you do business with. Think about your service providers; your colleagues; your customers; the restaurants you eat at; the stores you shop at. How many of them are consistently excellent? How many of them consistently sustain championship performance?

And what about you? What percent of the time are you at your best? Come on, think about last week. Think about last Monday, Tuesday, Wednesday, Thursday, Friday. Get a blank piece of paper and write down the five days, one underneath the other. Across the top of the page, write down four headings: mood, productivity, friendliness and excitement for each day. Now score yourself from 1-10 on each attribute.

How did you do? If you scored 170-200, you are a champion in consistency. If you scored 130-169, you are on the right side of the scale but you are still spending too much time in the negative zone. If you scored less than 130, you have some major work to do.

Everyday is World Cup Final Day!

You see, here's the point we're making in this session: Everyday is World Cup Final Day. Everyday could be the day! In fact, today may be the day you come face to face with the biggest opportunity of your life. And you may not even know it. How many opportunities do you think you've missed because you weren't at the top of your game when the moment demanded it? How many sales have you lost because you weren't excited or turned on? How many mistakes could you have avoided if you were in peak form at the time? How many actions or wasted chances do you regret because you just weren't up to it at the time?

Here's our message: In the highly competitive, take-no-prisoners environment of the new millennium, you cannot afford to snooze. You cannot afford to indulge in the luxury of an off-day. Your customers or colleagues don't care about your problems. They don't care if your wife has left you, or if the dog has gone missing or if your teenage son is giving you a hard time. They want you to deliver the goods. They want you to be there for them. They want you to inspire and enthuse them. You are the one who has to lift others up - day in and day out - with no time off for good behaviour.

Yup, it's brutal. But it's the price you have to pay if you want to be the best. And it's a price you have to pay willingly - with love and total commitment. It's worth it. The rewards are huge - both in financial and personal terms. What's more it gets easier over time. You know why? Because it becomes a habit. You develop your consistency fiber to the point where you do whatever it takes to succeed and help others do the same.

People who understand the power of consistency ultimately triumph over their competition. They know that life and business is not a sprint, it's a marathon. They know that one bad day can ruin a business. One action of neglect or carelessness can lose a valued customer. So they consciously guard against complacency or mediocrity. Do you?

When we do presentations to customers and prospects, we know that the only moment that matters is the one we're in right now. Yesterday's wins are history. Tomorrow's wins haven't yet happened. Today is all that counts. Today is the day that decides our destiny.

Today is our entire career in miniature. In fact, as you read this book, these words are the only connection between you and us. These words are either turning you onto us or off us. Not the words that you read on the previous page or the words that you'll read on the next page. This is it.

Every act carries with it the promise of greatness or the seeds of self-destruction. There is no such thing as an unimportant meeting, or an unimportant call or an unimportant customer. Everything you do is another piece of your character.

So let us ask you this vital question: Are your everyday actions, thoughts and habits consistently making you great, or they consistently making you mediocre? What can you change right now to achieve game excellence?

Take a blank piece of paper and write down ten things you are currently doing that you know are *decreasing* your personal power.

Now write down then things you can do right now that will increase your personal power.

Now make a vow to do what you have to do. Come on, read the following statement aloud and with conviction:

By the power vested in me by my Creator, I swear with all my heart and soul that I will do what I know I have to do to achieve my dream. I know I am destined for greatness and I will eliminate everything that stands in the way of my quest. I will honour myself with words and actions that maximize my potential. I will be all that I can and choose to be. I will take others along with me on my journey. So help me (your name).

Did you recite your vow? Did you do it with passion and conviction? If you didn't, do it now. Change the words if you want. The important point is that you constantly remind yourself to perform at your highest level because it's too easy to slack off or give up. You need to be your own best coach. You need to be your own best fan. You need to be your own 24 hour-a-day motivator. So write your own vow if you wish. Use the words that truly get your motor running. And then, keep your vow with you at all times. Say it to yourself and to others as often as you want.

Here's an interesting exercise: Get the people you work with to write their own personal vows. Get them to share it with you and with each other.

Then, write a group vow that everyone buys into. And reward people for living according to the vow.

What are we talking about here? We're talking about personal standards. We're talking about committing your heart and soul to outstanding, beyond-the-call-of-duty performance. Very often, the difference between making it and breaking it, comes down to personal commitment. The commitment to consistently delivering the goods no matter what.

One of the mistakes many entrepreneurs make is that they assume the people around them share their passion for the business. They assume their staff is naturally driven by the same dream as they are. Maybe not. Entrepreneurs who thrive over a sustained period of time, invest massive amounts of energy in ensuring all their people are imbued with the same spirit they have for the business. You see, customers buy more than goods or services from you, they buy feelings. The feeling they get from your frontline people is one of the most important reasons why they will stay with you or run away forever.

By the way, we are very interested in both your personal and group vows. If you wish, please visit www.mikelipkin.com and leave a message for us. We'll give you our insight and feedback.

Adopt a zero-excuse approach to life:

There is an ancient myth about the Greek General who invaded an island to capture a Queen he lusted after. As the last of his troops disembarked from the ships, he said to his second-in-command, "Burn the ships!!". The second-in-command responded anxiously, "But my general, if we burn the ships and we lose the battle, we'll be slaughtered!". To which the general replied with a smile, "EXACTLY!!" Needless to say, they won the battle and the General got his queen.

What's our point? If you burn your excuses, you have no choice but to make it happen. Failure is not an option. Even if you have setbacks(which you will), you treat them as temporary challenges that can only make you stronger.

We have seen so many people start off their venture fired up with enthusiasm only to lose it when their business hits turbulence. They start to look for reasons why the problems are not their fault. They start to blame others. They start to fall into the trap of victimhood. Their minds get stuck in There's-nothing-I can-do mode. They start having their own private self-pity parties. As a result, they lose their will. And the moment that happens, the end is a heartbeat away.

On the other hand, the winners turn their crises into triumph. They treat every tough moment as a defining moment. They know that it is how they handle their problems that will strengthen their entrepreneurial capacity or crush it. But there is no course on guts. There are no textbooks that can give you true grit. Character is not something you learn in a classroom. It's something you discover in the heat of battle when you're under fire.

You know what amazes us as we travel across this country motivating and empowering people? It's that two people can be faced with the same situation. One person will crack. They will panic. They will give in to their fear and fail. The other person, however, will rise to the occasion. They will reach deep down and tap into hidden reserves. They will become their best when things are at their worst. What kind of person are you in times of thunder? Will you fly with the angels? Or will you pack up shop?

Think about how you've performed in the past. How have you handled the pressure? Have people come to you for hope and inspiration? Did you hold your line when others were breaking for cover? Re-examine your past performance. It's a guide to how you'll act in the future. And you know what? Even if you aren't proud of some of your past deeds, it's okay. Human leopards can change their spots. But you have to make the commitment and you have to burn your excuses.

Both of us have hit heavy weather. Both of us have had moments where we wanted to give up. Both of us have walked through the valley of the shadow of death. We still have those moments now. And we know we will have those moments in the future. It's normal.

But you know what else we know? We will never, ever, ever, ever give-up. We will never extinguish the entrepreneurial dream that lights our path. Whatever pain awaits us, it's nothing compared to the immeasurable pleasure of a successful venture.

There is a saying we keep close to our hearts that has been a continual source of encouragement to both of us. We hope it will help you as well:

In times of scarcity, prepare for times of plenty.
In times of plenty, prepare for times of scarcity.

In other words, a zero-excuse approach to life prohibits you from pessimism or smugness. You can never lose hope but you can never lose fear. Somewhere between those two emotions is your personal high ground. If you've got the courage, you begin the journey to that place somewhere inside you.

Guarantee results through the mental preparation and ritual of champions

There is one technique common to great athletes: They mentally prepare for an event by going through their own unique ritual that gets them into the High Performance Zone. From now on, watch the great ones as they prepare for their events. Pay special attention to the little acts they perform. Read about what they do in the lead up towards to the event. You'll discover they all have a specific ritual. And if you want to hit your own maximum level of performance you have to do exactly the same.

In the previous section, we addressed the technique of visualization. But having your own high performance ritual empowers you with even greater consistency. Here's how it works: Think about those things you do that put you in a great mood. Maybe it's listening to music. Maybe it's listening to a motivational speaker. Maybe it's the way you get dressed in the morning; the clothes you wear; the food you eat; the exercise you do; the gestures you make. It could be any one of a thousand things. But it's something that turns you on. It's your own little ceremony that you perform that energizes you.

And the most important thing about this ritual is that you must do it everyday. The whole point of ritual and ceremony is to remind you to act with consciousness, to help you guard against taking anything for granted or become smug and complacent. That's why we pray in a certain way everytime we go into a church, mosque or synagogue. All religions are based on ritual. And one thing's for certain, if you are going to become an entrepreneur, you are going to have to treat your business like a religion. You are going to have to follow it with the same discipline, faith and belief.

Mike, for example, has delivered over 1000 motivational sessions over the past six years. He ascribes his consistent performance to the ritual he has developed over the years. Before each talk, Mike goes through the following 7 steps:

Firstly, some time before the session, he has to do strenuous exercise for 30 minutes or more. Mike needs the natural high provided by the endorphins produced by the brain during physical activity.

Secondly, he will not eat two hours before the event. He needs the feeling of lightness to dance with his audience.

Thirdly, he listens to some great music by James Brown, Aretha Franklin, Steppenwolf or George Benson.

Fourthly, He visualizes the session going extremely well. In fact, he visualizes every audience giving him a standing ovation and shouting, "Viva Lipkin, Viva!!" at the end of the session. At the same time, he concentrates on how much benefit he is going to provide the audience. He focuses on why this day will be a turning point for many people in the audience.

Fifthly, He exercises his face by saying certain words and putting his face through a range of different expressions. He also moves around physically alternating between shouting YES!! and breathing deeply.

Sixthly, he gets centred by concentrating on the calm and serenity inside himself.

Finally, he offers a silent prayer of thanks to his creator for allowing him to do what he does. He immerses himself in gratitude for the experience he is about to have.

What's your daily ritual? Do not proceed any further until you have thought about how you can get into the high performance zone before you get to work. Also, think about how you get your people into the Zone. Maybe it's a daily pep talk. Maybe it's a company song or chant. Maybe it's just a couple kind words to each person. Maybe it's tea and muffins. You decide.

C'mon, try it - even if you're sceptical. What have you got to lose? We promise you it works.

The Art of Remarkable Recovery:

How to make your mistakes really work for you

"Even Monkeys fall out of trees"   *Old Japanese proverb*

If you are the kind of person who first of all bought this book and then made it this far, you are one of those people who hold themselves to a higher standard. You are also the kind of person who is hard on themselves when a mistake is made. You find it difficult to forgive yourself for making mistakes. And, the chances are, you find it as difficult to forgive others for their mistakes.

Well, here's the truth: If you're an entrepreneur, especially a successful entrepreneur, you're going to make mistakes and you're going to make lots of them.

And here's another truth: A mistake can be the most beneficial experience you ever have as long as you forgive yourself for it, learn from it and move on.

Let us ask you this question: Over the past six months, have you done anything you think was stupid? Have you done anything that you think made you look stupid? Do you look back at some of the things you've done and still feel the flush of embarrassment? We know the answer is yes to all these questions. What's our point? All of us do stupid things. We are all fallible. We're all human beings. And human beings are not computers. We do not run with the efficiency of a quartz watch. Even the best of us, screw up and screw up big.

"Can you meet with Triumph and Disaster and treat those two imposters just the same."?

We promise you that all the great entrepreneurs through the centuries have made mistakes. They have lost fortunes almost as quickly as they made them. Their common denominator, however, was their ability to use their mistakes as powerful learning experiences. They didn't allow the mistakes to fester into personal failures. They never lost their fighting spirit. In fact for many of them, including us, their mistakes strengthened their resolve. While others went to ground and waited for the storm to blow over, they came out with all guns blazing. Read the biographies of Ray Krok(McDonalds), Colonel Saunders(Kentucky Fried Chicken), Lee Iacocca(Chrysler), Robbie Brozin(Nando's), Herman Mashaba(Black Like Me), Anant Singh(Cry, the Beloved Country), Raymond Ackerman(Pick 'n Pay) and Eric Molobi (Kagiso). You'll find out that mistakes are the real currency of achievement. And the bigger the mistakes, the bigger the ultimate achievement.

In fact, we don't even use the word "mistake" any more. We use the words "unexpected results". That's why we don't make mistakes any more, we just get unexpected results. And as Tom Peters says, the unexpected results from any action will always outnumber the expected results.

So how do you currently handle mistakes or unexpected results? Are you the kind of person who loses their temper often? Do you make your colleagues' lives miserable when they slip or stumble? Do you blow small things out of proportion? Are you a source of tension during tough times?

Or are you the kind of person who, in the immortal words of Rudyard Kipling, "can meet with Triumph and Disaster and treat those two imposters just the same."?

The ability to handle misfortune, setbacks, losses, injustices, rejection, or simple slumps is central to being a successful entrepreneur. Kipling was right. He didn't know it but he was describing the essential trait of an entrepreneur. You know why? Because nothing is permanent. Everything is in constant change. Today's triumph is tomorrow's disaster. In fact, one of the biggest causes of failure is success. When people become successful, they run the risk of losing their humility, hunger or energy.

So, here's a daring exercise for you to test your RQ - your Recovery Quotient: In the next ten days, do something that you've never done before. Go where you've never been before. Do something before you're a 100% ready to do it. Take a walk on the wild side. Step over the line of safety. Break the Comfort Barrier. Feel what it's like to get unexpected results. Get used to it. You know what will happen? For every "mistake" you will get at least two breakthroughs. You'll experience a liberation from self-doubt and uncertainty. You'll become more decisive. You'll begin to taste the exhilaration of being your own boss!

The key to managing any mistake: What is, is. What was, was. What will be, will be. Accept and advance.

Wherever you are, that's where you're supposed to be right now. Whatever has happened to you had to happen to you because it did happen to you. Whatever problems you face, you have the power to deal with them - although you may not realize it yet. That's the key to mastering any mistake: What is, is. What was, was, what will be, will be. Accept and advance.

We've met so many people who are eating themselves up alive over something that has happened yesterday. They are immobilised by the past. They cannot move forward because they cannot accept what has happened. As a result, everyday they commit suicide by installment. They shrink into the future and die broken and disillusioned.

Great entrepreneurs, on the other hand, have the remarkable ability to accept what has happened and move on. They are future focused. They are action oriented. They don't waste precious energy on what cannot be changed. They invest all of themselves on what can.

So here's a powerful exercise for you to do right now. Take a piece of paper and divide it into three columns:

In the first column, write down the three biggest mistakes you think you've ever made when it comes to your career - one underneath the other.

In the second column, next to each of the three mistakes, write down why this mistake was so bad for your career.

Now, in the third column - next to each mistake, write down why it could have been the best thing to ever happen to you. Be serious about this column - it's your passport to the future. Unless you can truly believe that everything that has happened to you serves you, you cannot move forward.

In the 2000's, we're all going to have to travel light. We're going to have move fast. He who hesitates is not only lost but miles from the next opportunity. Carrying emotional and mental baggage around with you is an indulgence no-one can afford. The world owes you zero. It will give you whatever you want, but you have to earn it through guts, grit and brains.

Finally, take a deep breadth and say aloud, *"I bless and let go of these mistakes. I choose to use my past to focus on my future. I am thankful for having made it this far. I look forward to making my future great. I accept what cannot be changed. I have the courage to change what I can. Yes!!"*

A mistake is simply an opportunity to recover magnificently so you can make Raving Fans.

Ken Blanchard, the well known management author, coined the term "Raving Fans". A Raving Fan is someone who is so delighted by what you've done for them, or how you've treated them, that they rave about you to whoever they meet. A Raving Fan is a walking, talking, live commercial for you and your services.

We promise you that your livelihood and our livelihood depend on the number of Raving Fans we all have. Even the sales of this book depend on how many people talk about it enthusiastically after reading it. That's why we are packing the best of what we know into every page. We want to turn you into a Raving Fan. And by the way, let us know if you've become a Raving fan by leaving a message on www.mikelipkin.com.

So how many Raving Fans do you have? How many of your customers are walking around raving about you to everyone they meet? Are you even consciously pursuing this objective? Because we promise you, there can be no more important business objective than delighted customers raving about how outstanding you are.

So what have Raving Fans got to do with making mistakes? Plenty. As sure as all of us have only a limited time on this planet, so we will all make mistakes. It's how you recover from your mistakes that will determine the health of your customer relationships. A mistake with a customer can be the beginning of the end or it can be the start of a new beginning. Time and time again we see business people failing because they treated a mistake as a defeat or a reason to get defensive.

Or, even worse, they tried to avoid the customer. They ran away because they couldn't deal with the confrontation.

Here's a powerful secret of highly successful entrepreneurs: Every mistake is a massive opportunity to recover magnificently so you can make Raving Fans. If there's one thing that everyone admires, it's the ability to come back from a mistake. People love to read about come-back stories. In fact, people need these stories because they're proof that there's always hope.

Now look, we're not saying that you can afford to keep making mistakes day in and day out and still be successful. In fact, if you've ever made the same mistake twice, it means you're not learning. Or, if the mistake was made out of negligence or carelessness, it's a bad mistake that will get you nowhere. The mistakes we're talking about are the mistakes made in the spirit of innovation, speed and exploration. And they are new mistakes - the currency of the future.

Our 4 step formula for recovering magnificently so you can make Raving Fans

So let's say you make a mistake and you let a customer down. Have you ever had this kind of experience? If you're reading these words, we know you have. What should you do? Well, think about the last time this happened to you, what did you do? In fact, right now, write down your experience under four headings:

The Mistake.
The Clients'/marketplace's response.
The action you took.
The results.

How did you feel when you made the mistake? How did the customer respond? How did you handle the client? What results did you achieve? Did you succeed in strengthening the relationship? Or was the relationship impaired forever? Here is our 4 step formula for recovering magnificently so you can make Raving Fans:
Immediately accept responsibility for the mistake. Don't blame the customer, the supplier or your employees.
Put yourself in the client's shoes and empathize with their feelings.

Ask yourself what you would be feeling if it had happened to you.
Ask yourself what action you need to take to completely turn around
the customer's negative feelings into overwhelmingly favourable
ones. Do whatever it takes. Spare no expense.

Take action. Let the customer know exactly what you're doing. Let the
customer know how much value they're getting. Commit to
outstanding service delivery in the future follow up.

Treat the customer as a VIRGI

At the end of the day, there are only two emotions, which really drive
all of us: the need to be accepted and the need to be recognized as
someone special. Often, customers respond negatively to a mistake
because they believe they are being taken for granted, or that you
don't really care, or that this is just another demonstration of how
horrible their life has become.

How many times has someone responded to you with a rage out of
all proportion to the mistake that was made? In fact, how many times
have you been guilty of this action? Well, we believe it's not the cause
of the outburst that matters, it's what's going on in the customer's life
at the time of the incident.

So here's the Golden Rule: Don't take it personally. Don't respond
to a customer's outburst with an outburst of your own. Rather, recycle
the customer's negative energy into a positive force by treating them
as a VIRGI - Very Important Revenue Generator Infinitum. Even while
the customer is venting their frustration on you, see into the future.
See this very customer raving about you to others because of how you
handled this problem. See this customer as your number one future
revenue generator. And watch the difference.

None of us can afford to have people running around
badmouthing us. We cannot afford to have people telling other people
not to do business with us. In a service business, all we really have is
our reputations. So while there will always be some people who don't
buy into you or us, we all have to be extremely vigilant that we don't
make enemies for nothing.

Remember one of the fundamental laws of wealth: *It's better to be
rich than it is to be right.*

The importance of leisure and re-creation: all work and no play makes you blind, blunt and boring:

One of the biggest risks you face as an entrepreneur is burnout.

You put yourself on the line. You commit everything you have to the business. You cannot afford to fail. You work harder and harder to make your venture a success. The pressure gets heavier and heavier. Your work hours get longer and longer. You live, breathe, eat, sleep your business. And before you know it, you begin to lose your edge. You become irritable. Small things begin to bug you. You find it harder and harder to generate the enthusiasm you need to motivate your staff. Your work becomes a grudge activity instead of pleasure. You are starting to pay the price of not taking time-out.

Like any machine, the human mind and body needs regular tune-ups and servicing. If you keep driving your mind and body harder and harder, they're going to crack up on you. Just like they cracked up on Mike. As you read in the introduction to the book, Mike has his triple Ph.D. in failure, burnout and depression. If there is one thing that Mike's experience taught him, it's the importance of dedicating time to recharging your batteries and re-energizing yourself.

Taking time off from the business is not being lazy. It's not being irresponsible, it's vital! Your sustained success depends on your ability to keep on going through all kinds of weather; it depends on your ability to stay sharp and alert; it depends on your ability to carry others through the hard times. And you simply cannot perform if you are mentally and physically weary.

You see, it's not the stress that gets to you. It's the lack of escape from stress. Unless you leave the forest occasionally, you'll never see the wood for the trees. Unless you step out of the pressure cooker every now and then, you'll explode. Like heart disease, constant stress clogs up your mental arteries without you even being aware of it until it's too late.

So here's our question, what are you doing to re-create and rejuvenate yourself? How are you keeping yourself young and vigorous in mind and body? We promise you, your leisure and relaxation activities are just as important as the time you spend at work. We talk to so many entrepreneurs who are already managing their own businesses. We see some of them light up a cigarette or have a couple drinks too many. We see them overeat and put on weight. And when we ask them why they don't take care of themselves physically, they tell us - "We don't have the time!".

For these entrepreneurs, physical and mental well being is not a priority. They are taking their health for granted. They are wearing down their resources. Until, one day - WHAMMO!! The sickness hits. Maybe it's a heart attack or maybe it's depression or maybe it's the Big C or maybe something somewhere in the body ceases to function. Then, all of a sudden, they catch a wake-up call - when the damage is done.

We are all athletes

If you're a professional cricket player or soccer player or rugby player, maybe your career will last five years, maybe seven, maybe even ten if you're lucky. But if you're a businessperson who wants to become an entrepreneur, your career can span 30-40 years.

The bottom line is that just like sportspeople, entrepreneurs are athletes. Your business will place enormous demands on your mental and physical resources. If you don't develop them with discipline, they'll disappear. You know why? Because whatever you don't use, you lose.

Mike's re-creation and rejuvenation activities

As a motivator and corporate coach, Mike makes sure he works out six days a week. He alternates between running and swimming. He is extremely careful about what he eats and keeps to a low fat diet. He loves movies and goes to at least one a week. He makes sure he spends enough quality time with his family and especially his six year old daughter, Dani-Emma who is his role model. Mike also gets away five to six times a year on "mini-breaks". These are 3-4 day getaways rather than one long break over the hectic in-season period. Mike will also attend at least two seminars a year on high performance and motivation. He reads a book and 15 magazines a week. Finally, Mike ensures that he spends as much time as possible with "magic" people. These are people who are as turned on as he is. They feed him with energy and inspiration and he returns the favour.

Eric's re-creation and rejuvenation activities

Eric's recreation time is spent with the special people who recharge his batteries - close friends and family. He has a joint share in a holiday home in Mbona in the Natal Midlands. It is an unwritten law in Eric's life that he must go to Mbona at least once a month to rest, recreate and rejuvenate. Eric is also a sports-lover both as spectator and player with soccer and cricket being his two favourites. Like Mike, Eric is an avid reader. But it is the business pages that he follows with special interest - everyday may bring with it a new opportunity.

The ultimate entrepreneurial social exam: Do you pass the Pavlov's Dog Test? Do you make people salivate?

Have you heard of Ivan Pavlov? He was the scientist who discovered the true meaning of the word, "conditioning". What did he do? Well, he fed this dog. And every time he fed the dog, he rang a bell. After five weeks, he asked the dog if it knew what it was eating. "No" it replied, "But its name rings a bell!"

Seriously, what did the dog do when it heard the bell, even when there was no food in front of him? It salivated because it had associated the sound of bell with food. So here's the million dollar question: **When people hear your name, do they salivate?** Do they drool? Do they associate you with pleasure? Or do they groan? Do they associate you with pain? Or, even worse, do they feel nothing towards you?

Here's a timeless law of business success: *People do business with people they enjoy doing business with.* So as you read these words, think of your most important customer. Pretend that they are thinking of you right now. Are they filled with a sense of pleasurable anticipation? Do they consider you a friend? Are you a source of inspiration and advice for them? If the answer to any of these questions is "no" then maybe you fail the ultimate entrepreneurial social exam.

And the only way you'll pass the ultimate entrepreneurial exam is by staying vibrant yourself. As an independent businessperson, you have to be the source of inspiration to everyone around you. You have no safety net or security blanket. You are the safety net and security blanket to others. So make sure you spend as much time on your personal motivation and health plan as you do on your businessplan.

Courageous Creativity: How to combine guts and innovation to solve problems, discover new solutions, think laterally and generate options.

Courageous: The Quality of mind or spirit that enables one to face extreme dangers and difficulties with firmness and without fear.

Creativity: To cause to come into being something unique that would not normally evolve or that is not made by ordinary processes; to evolve from one's thoughts or imagination; to make by investing with new functions

Webster's Dictionary

As an entrepreneur, there will always be two qualities that will be required from you at all times: courage and creativity. If we can guarantee you one thing, it's that no matter how successful you become, you will always be confronted with two challenges:

Firstly, how do you stay courageous in the face of dangers that would crush lesser mortals?

Secondly, How do you sustain your creativity to produce new products or improve existing ones in the face of competitive pressure and customer demands?

One of the most successful businesspeople in the world, Warren Buffet - Chairman of Berkshire Hathaway, one of the ten most admired companies in the America (Fortune Magazine, March 1 1999) - said, "I am not a businessman, I am an artist". We believe that Buffet has summed up the most important quality of the 21st Century entrepreneur - creativity. Specifically creativity as defined by the Webster's Dictionary: **To cause to come into being something unique that would *not normally* evolve or that is *not made by ordinary processes*.**

How many times have you been exposed to a new business concept that impressed you and said to yourself, "That's amazing"? Well, we believe that the main difference between an entrepreneur and a manager is the ability to create new things or invest existing things with new functions that provide a new and unique benefit to customers.

The second main difference between entrepreneurs and managers is their level of courage. We like the Webster's definition of courageous because it highlights the need for "firmness". You cannot expect to become great by losing your nerve or becoming indecisive in the face of extreme challenges. Crises call for a Command Mentality. If you are going to take on the Unknown, you have to take it on with a spirit of boldness.

And by the way, when Webster's says being courageous means being without fear, we believe they mean the "bad fear". The "bad fear" is panic, uncertainty and doubt.

So, the main intent of this session is to show you how to develop courage and creativity to solve problems, discover new solutions, think laterally and generate options. Let's go!

We all have the Picasso inside. What's yours??

Picasso was the greatest artist of the 20th Century. His paintings have sold for over R20 million each. He was a creative genius. And you know what? So are you!

Picasso was a creative genius when it came to painting or drawing pictures. But we promise you that you are a genius at something as well. Your personal mission as an entrepreneur is to discover and develop that genius to its highest level. If you focus on that mission with unshakeable determination, you will become successful.

So Mike believes that his genius is communicating through the written and spoken word. Everything he does is aimed at developing this genius, including this book. Eric believes that his genius is connecting, understanding and helping others achieve their goals, and that's why he is involved with this book.

It is so vital for you to discover your inner Picasso because otherwise you cannot truly be creative. If you are not following the right path for you, your journey will end up at the wrong destination. So think deeply about what you believe you can be a genius at. And then follow that genius with firmness and desire.

The seed of all creativity: Intuition

The dictionary has some stunning definitions of Intuition: *direct perception of the truth; a keen and quick insight; pure untaught knowledge; immediate understanding.*

All great entrepreneurs are highly intuitive. They have a well developed 6th sense that alerts them to opportunities and solutions that others just don't see. They somehow "know" the answer by listening to a little voice inside their heads. Have you ever heard this "inner voice"? Have you ever just known what to do even though you couldn't quite explain it afterwards? Have you wanted to do something but heard a voice inside your head saying, "Don't go there!"?

We're sure that your answer to all these questions is yes, yes, yes! The difference, however, between successful entrepreneurs and failures, is that the successes have the guts to honour their intuition and act on it. Some wise person once said, "Prayer is our way of talking to God. Intuition is God's way of talking to us".

So how do you develop your Intuition? Slowly. Over time, be alert to the messages your inner voice is sending you. Listen to your "gut feel". Have the courage to do what you believe you have to do even if it means taking the harder option. And, if something doesn't feel right to you, don't do it, no matter how much pressure others are applying to you.

Now you can see why it's so much easier to develop your intuition if you are following your genius. You see, if you are following your genius, all your senses are in tune with you. You are doing what you were meant to do. You are operating at a higher level. You are programmed to notice what you need to notice. But, on the other hand, if you are not following your genius, you will be out of alignment. You won't be in the Zone. You will struggle and stumble into nowhere.

If the seed of all creativity is intuition, then excitement is its fertilizer

Quick, right now, think about something that makes you very excited. Maybe it has something to do with your existing business; maybe it's what you've already learnt in this book; maybe it's the business you're about to start; maybe it's a holiday you're about to go on; maybe it's somebody who really winds your clock. Whatever it is, think about anything that makes you very, very excited. In fact, how would you feel right now, if we told you that you had just won R1,000,000 tax free in the national lottery?

Notice what happens to you when you get excited: You become energized; you want to move around; you want to share your enthusiasm with others; you become animated and motivated. You also become clever. Your brain starts to hum at a higher frequency. Your mind starts to kick into overdrive.

We promise you that when you become excited, you become creative. If you are not turned on, you will not maximize your creativity. Notice that when you are in a bad mood, you are devoid of great ideas; you aren't motivated to stretch your brain to come up with new options; in fact, when you're in a bad mood - you're probably going to be stupid!

So get excited, stay excited and help others become excited. After speaking to literally thousands of entrepreneurs, we believe that the make-or-break quality for success is the ability to excite oneself and others. Excited people are creative people. And excited, creative people always beat their competition to the punch.

Now we know what you may be thinking: How do I get and stay excited all the time? Well, it's simple but it takes practice. It's called the 7 Questions of Excitement. You need to ask them multiple times a day. You need to get the people around you to ask these questions. And as you ask these questions, you need to genuinely believe in the answers:

The 7 Questions of Excitement
1. Who have I helped today?
2. What have I learned today?
3. How have I got closer to my dream today?
4. What is the nicest thing that has happened to me today?

5. Why should I be excited about tomorrow, today?
6. Who are the people who have given me their love and support today?
7. How come I got so lucky to have what I have today?

As you answer the 7 Questions of Excitement, focus only on positive answers to the questions. Do not allow negativity or cynicism to enter your heart and mind. Let in your excitement and your creativity will follow.

Practical techniques for becoming creative: Nine tried and tested paths to innovation:

1. *Truly believe that you are creative in your specific field.* One of the biggest obstacles to creativity is that people do not really believe they are creative. And if you do not believe that you are truly creative, you won't be. It's as simple as that. Henry Ford once said, "If you believe you can do it. Or you believe you can't do it. You're right!".

Successful entrepreneurs go into their business with an unshakeable belief in their ability to find solutions or solve problems that no-one else can. They absolutely believe that there is no mountain too high for them to climb. And every time they reach their peak, they look for a higher mountain to climb.

2. *Always expect the unexpected.* Tom Peters, the well known management consultant, said, "The unexpected results of every action will always outnumber the expected results". Entrepreneurs are always looking for the unusual to happen. They know that life is full of surprises and so they are not surprised by life. Instead, they thrive on the unexpected. They seize opportunities as they arise.

That's one of the reasons why we are writing this book together. Government's policies and corporate strategies are unexpectedly moving in the same direction. Affirmative action and private sector downsizing are forcing a mass of talented people to become job creators not job seekers. This is building momentum with unprecedented speed. It's also causing massive amounts of stress among individuals who have been placed in this situation. So while there are many books on how to start your own business, we believe there is nothing on the market as comprehensive as this book.

It was amazing, but in the light of what's happening in South Africa, both Eric and Mike wanted to write a book for entrepreneurs at the same time. Then Mike read an article about Eric in the financial press and immediately called him with the book proposal. Eric agreed instantly and this whole book was written and published in under three months - a feat previously considered impossible in the South African publishing industry.

So ask yourself right now, what unexpected things could happen in your industry? If something unexpected happened right now, are you equipped to respond to it? How fast can you move? Who would you approach to move with you? What can you do right now to prepare for the unexpected? Are your people ready?

3. *Think about your challenges from a completely different angle: Think outside the box. Challenge assumptions, especially your own.* Creative people have the ability to see things from a totally different perspective. They ask questions other people don't ask and so they get answers other people don't get.

For example, what's the biggest problem facing you in your work right now? C'mon, think about the one predicament that you are finding unsolvable right now. Think about how you have been thinking about it. Now, look at the problem from a completely different angle. Now change the angle again, and come up with another different way of redefining the problem.

Here's an example of how we thought about this book from a completely different angle. In South Africa, authors do not really make money from books. That's because of the size of the royalty they get from book sales. Furthermore, the author cannot really control the marketing of the book because that's up to the publisher. In addition, the production and publishing of the book is also a long drawn out process.

So we looked at the problem from a completely different angle. We asked ourselves, "Why don't we play the role of authors and publishers?". We thought, "We can raise money for the book through sponsorships. We are both connected enough to get the bookstores to support us. We are both marketers so we'll find ways to market the book. We'll find ways to warehouse and distribute the book. And, we'll produce this book lightning fast." And, presto, you're reading the end product.

So today, challenge the assumptions of everyone around you, as well as your own. If someone tells you it can't be done, ask why. And then, show them why not. Take nothing for granted. Ask new questions. Ask crazy questions. Ask, "what If?" We promise you, eventually, you'll find a way or make a way even when others say there is no way.

4. *Sleep on it: Let your subconscious mind sort it out for you.* We want to ask you these questions: Have you ever been faced with a problem that you didn't know how to solve? And no matter how hard you thought about it, you just couldn't come up with a solution? And, then, one day while you were doing something else, the answer just popped into your head? Well, what happened was that your subconscious was working on the problem all the time.

So sometimes you literally just have to sleep on it. If you hit a mental block, don't force it. Relax. Say to yourself, "*I now hand this problem over to my subconscious to sort out for me. I know that I have the answer deep down. I will give my mind time to find out and bring it up to me.*" Whatever happens, don't panic and don't become anxious. Panic and anxiety will only push your creativity further and further away.

Try it this evening. Before you go to sleep, think about the biggest challenge facing you right now. Ask your subconscious to work on it while you sleep. You'll be amazed at the results you get. Here's a tip, though, you can't expect this technique to work all the time. Your mind is not like a vending machine. The solutions will not pop out on demand. Although, the more you practice this technique, the more successful you will become.

5. *Be open to everything. Sharpen your senses. Seek inspiration and learning everywhere.* Highly creative people have open minds. Their senses are tuned to all the stimuli around them. They are constantly searching for inspiration everywhere they go. Life is one long learning system for them. They expect to find solutions and ideas in unlikely places and so they do.

Here are some examples of how ideas were discovered by open thinkers, whose senses were alert to the possibilities of life:
Radar came from studying reflected soundwaves from flying bats; Velcro was invented by studying the way certain weeds stuck to

clothing; Cat's eyes in the road come from studying the way light was reflected by real cat's eyes; ball and socket joints came from studying animal skeletons; Frozen foods were discovered by a man who travelled to Canada and noticed that salmon which were frozen in ice, tasted fresh when they thawed.

How open are you to the possibilities around you? Mike is constantly being inspired by everything around him because that's how he makes a living - by telling stories about real life in South Africa. Every personal experience is therefore an opportunity to develop new material for his seminars and books.

6. *Expose yourself to as many new people and ideas as possible.* Both of us are continually flying around the world attending conferences, delivering seminars, meeting people, reading books and trade magazines, and being exposed to new ideas. In fact, almost everything you read in this book is a result of the inspiration and input we have received as a result of our activities. We see ourselves as "knowledge recyclers".

Are you speaking to as many people as possible? Do you belong to trade associations? Are you a member of a charity group like the Rotary Club or the Lion's Club? Are you reading as much as possible, not just about your industry but about anything in general? Do you go out of your way to meet and speak with people who may come from a very different background to you?

Remember, the more you stimulate your brain cells, the more active they become. The brain is like any other muscle in your body: It needs to be consistently stimulated. You need to read. You need to think. You need to engage in active debate with smart people. Just like an athlete, you need to train your mind vigorously if it is to perform well.

And most importantly, engage your staff in dialogue. Encourage them to speak up. South Africans tend to be hesitant to speak up. You need to create a climate of openness and trust so your people feel licensed to speak their mind. You'll be amazed at what you can discover from them.

7. *Suspend judgement. Don't shoot down ideas until you've had a chance to consider them carefully.* One of the biggest obstacles to

creativity is our natural tendency to criticize people and ideas before we have really given them a chance. Think about how many times you've judged something or someone harshly only to discover later that you were in the wrong.

So refrain from judgement until you've considered another person's idea from every angle. In fact, start off by presuming they are right. Give them the benefit of whatever doubt you may have. You know what else will happen if you do this? You will gain a reputation as someone who is willing to listen. People will seek you out to share their ideas with you. And before you know it, you'll hit the creative jackpot - you'll find the "Big Idea" and run with it.

8. Be tenacious. Hang in there. Never, ever, ever give up. Truly creative people have the ability to keep going when everyone else has thrown in the towel. They refuse to let go of their vision. Sometimes, they are so persistent that other people may call them stubborn or even stupid. But they know the answer is out there so they keep searching.

The "Big Idea" will very rarely present itself to you first time round, or second time round or even third or fourth time round. That's why there are so few people who consistently demonstrate a high degree of creativity. It's because they can't or won't go the distance. They get demoralized or disheartened too easily. When the solution doesn't present itself to them soon enough, they stop searching, often when the answer is just around the corner.

Did you know that the Wright Brothers tried over 800 times before they achieved sustained flight? And did you know that Colonel Saunders approached over 1000 restaurants before he found someone who was willing to try his "secret" recipe of herbs and spices? And did you know that Sylvester Stallone approached over 100 agents before his script for "Rocky" was produced?

So how perseverant are you? Remember, God's delays are not God's denials - They are just a test to separate the truly committed from the merely interested. Often, just having the ability to keep searching when everyone else has stopped will give you the competitive advantage. If you truly believe in your quest, and your intuition tells you there's a better way, then find it.

Warning: Don't pour good money or time after bad. By that we mean, use your good judgement to determine whether you're heading down a cul-de-sac or blind alley. Don't confuse perseverance with blindness. The moment it becomes clear that what you are doing isn't going anywhere, change direction. Flexibility is the saving grace of successful entrepreneurs.

9. *Learn to live with change and uncertainty.* And that takes courage. Highly creative people thrive in times of chaos and uncertainty. You know why? Because they view change as a source of stimulation and new ideas, not as a threat or danger to their status or position. If you want to be creative, you have to make change your friend. And that's good news for all of us because change is going to happen anyway.

Successful entrepreneurs are at their best when change is at its biggest. They know that change shakes loose opportunities from the establishment. And that's why we believe South Africa is a dreamland for entrepreneurs right now. Like the Impala in the Kruger National Park, it's teeming with possibilities that are absent in the more established economies of Europe, North America and Australia.

But it takes courage. Times of change, uncertainty and turbulence are scary times. They are tough times. They make people afraid to take action because the consequences can be severe. Know this truth: *Everytime you want to innovate, you threaten someone who doesn't want change to happen.* Many people would rather die than change because it takes less effort. So expect resistance to your ideas and prepare for it in advance.

However, during times of change, uncertainty and turbulence, people also look for leadership and inspiration. They look for those companies that radiate a sense of purpose, quality, value and caring. Start one of those companies and you will thrive in the next millennium.

The Ultimate Leadership Skill:
Maximizing and actualizing the potential of everyone and everything around you.

"If you ever say you've arrived, you're dead"
Yul Brynner

Potential: Capable of being or becoming; a latent excellence that may or may not be developed.
Webster's Dictionary

As you can see from the cover of this book, Mike shares a common hairstyle with the late, great actor, Yul Brynner. However, Mike is a fan of Yul Brynner for many reasons. One of these reasons is Yul's attitude to life and his career. Once upon a time, a reporter asked Yul Brynner what he wanted on his tombstone. Brynner replied simply, "I've arrived!". When the reporter asked him why he wanted those words, Brynner responded, "Because if you ever say you've arrived, you're dead". We believe that those nine words sum up the entire attitude of this book.

We also both believe in the following truth: *Success is the biggest cause of failure but failure is the biggest reason for ultimate success.* In other words, don't let either success or failure go to your head. Learn both their lessons well.

After interacting with thousands of this country's most successful entrepreneurs over the past five years, we have discovered one golden thread that runs through all of them: However successful they are, they all believe that their best is yet to come. They have an enthusiasm and energy that is almost childlike in its glee. When we ask them about the future, they respond with passion and possibility. They tell us of their plans and how they hope to gain market share, increase sales and take their companies to the next level. What's more, although they may not like the chaos, crime or uncertainty, they never use the environment as an excuse not to perform. If anything, outside challenges just strengthen their determination to succeed.

The ultimate human tragedy

There is nothing more common in this world than wasted talent. Everyday, talented people trudge through life being less than they can be. They are miserable, bored, unfulfilled and frustrated. They know that there must be more to their life but they just can't seem to find the path to a better one. Maybe it's because they're not really looking. Or maybe it's because they've given up. Or maybe it's because they don't believe there is a better way.

Here's the ultimate human tragedy: If you don't develop your potential, your potential wastes away. Like any living thing, if you don't feed it, it dies. And there are so many people in South Africa today whose potential is dying because it's not being nurtured. Maybe it's because these people are just struggling to survive. Or maybe it's because their past has taken over their future. Or maybe it's because they don't have anyone around them to stimulate their dreams.

Well, here's the message of this session: The most successful entrepreneurs are pure potential-in-motion. They have one foot in the present and another in the immediate future. They are constantly growing into their next state of development. They never stand still. And they never become complacent. They are always fired up with a sense of possibility. It's like they are always stretching for the finishing line although they know there is no finishing line.

And do you know the most wonderful thing about these entrepreneurs? They take others along with them for the ride. Adam Smith, the pioneering economist who lived 200 years ago, called it the "Invisible Hand". He said that these entrepreneurs, in seeking their own dream, helped others find theirs.

Maximizer and Actualizer of Human Potential Test

So, are you a Maximizer and Actualizer of Human Potential, including your own? Do the following ten-point test to find out (rate yourself out of ten on each attribute):

1. Do you see things and automatically think of ways to improve them? _____
2. Are you constantly looking for new opportunities, no matter where you are? _____
3. Do you get immense pleasure out of watching people grow? _____
4. Are you always helping people do things better? _____
5. Do you get very excited when you think of new possibilities? _____
6. Do you want to grow or improve things just for the sake of it? _____
7. Are you good at teaching people and transferring knowledge? _____
8. Do you have a track record as an innovator and coach? _____
9. Are you constantly anticipating change or the next trend and taking action to exploit it? _____
10. In the past six months, have you helped at least six people grow or implemented at least six innovative concepts? _____

Total _____

If you scored 85+, you are a born developer of human potential. This session will merely fine-tune your God-given gift.

If you scored 71-84, you are moving in the right direction and this session will accelerate your progress.

If you scored less than 71, this session will show you how to develop this vital attribute of highly successful entrepreneurs.

The Power Of Anticipation:
The Number One Skill for the Millennium

The ancient biblical quote says, "Feed a man a fish and you feed him for a day. Teach a man to fish and you feed him for a lifetime" We say, "Give that man to us and we'll show him how to open a chain of seafood stores".

When you look at an acorn, what do you see? Do you see squirrel food? Do you see a tree? Do you see a forest? Or do you see all the houses that will be built from the forest that springs from the acorn?

Why are we asking you these questions? Simply because highly successful entrepreneurs are always thinking 5-10 moves ahead of their competition. They have the ability to see what something can become. They practice the power of anticipation. And then, as importantly, they take action. That's why they are always ahead of their competition. To quote Rudyard Kipling's words:

They copied all they could follow,
But they couldn't follow my mind;
And I left them sweating and stealing,
A year and a half behind

So, right now, think about a development or trend in your industry. Think carefully about the forces of change that are at work around you. Identify three trends or forces of change. Now think about where these trends or forces are going. Think one year down the track, think two years down the track, think five years down the track. Speak to people around you. Speak to suppliers; speak to customers; speak to competitors. Then think about what you can do now to capitalize on these trends. Then take action.

That's exactly how this book came about. We saw the forces of downsizing, privatization, affirmative action, increasing global entrepreneurial activity, the internet and changing attitudes towards work. We spoke to the large companies. We spoke to people who had been retrenched or who just can't find work. We spoke to students. We spoke to existing entrepreneurs. We spoke to banks, universities and schools. We spoke to the retail trade. We looked at what was currently on the market. We studied what was going on elsewhere in the world and then we took action.

So be an IAA, an Immediate Action Anticipator. Act with foresight. But act with urgency. See the gap. Then go for the gap. Yes, you need to look before you leap. But you also need to take that leap of faith before you've got all your ducks in a row. When we decided to write this book, we didn't know exactly what would be in it or how we would market it. All we knew was that we were staring at a big opportunity and that we had to act fast. Remember, it's better to be roughly right and first, than exactly right and suck hind-tit.

If you are going to be an actualizer and maximizer of human potential you need to be a PWB – A Person Without Borders

There is a social tidal wave sweeping over the world. It's caused by technology, democracy, mobility and our common humanity. It's the wave that is washing away national and cultural boundaries. The best talent and ideas rule. It doesn't matter where the talent or the ideas come from. So the new class of successful entrepreneurs will be PWB – People Without Borders. They will go where the opportunities are greatest and they will take from where the talent and ideas are most plentiful. They do not limit their vision to industry or geography. They are open, adaptable and mobile.

What are we saying to you here? Simply this, don't limit your vision. Get rid of any beliefs or rules that aren't serving you anymore. Re-examine all that you've been told. Challenge whatever you may have learnt in the past. This takes courage. It means you may have to discard certain things that you've believed in your whole life. Do it. And do it now. You are the captain of your own ship and you can take your ship anywhere you want to.

Do You Pass The Make-Or-Break Test of Personal Leadership?

Throughout history, people have laughed at, ridiculed and tried to put down people who were pioneers. Whenever someone introduces something new or goes where no-one else has ever been before, others will try to stop them or discourage them. Sometimes people will try and stop pioneers through good intentions. Maybe your friends and family don't want to see you fail. Other times, people will try and stop you because they are envious or threatened. Whatever the motivation, your resolve will be put to the test. You will be forced to go with your gut against the opinions or wishes of others.

And that's the Make-or-Break Test of Personal Leadership: Do you trust yourself enough to go with your own flow? Are you willing to zig when others say you should zag? Are you willing to swim against the popular current? Are you willing to put it all on the line in the face of fear and failure?

And are you able to persuade others to come for the ride with you? You see, it's one thing to persuade yourself. It's quite another to persuade others to join you in your quest. So, firstly, you need to come to terms with your challenge in your own mind. Then you need to ask yourself what you need to do to get others to embrace the challenge with you.

That's how we managed to get the sponsors to join us in producing this book. We knew this book was the right initiative at the right time in the right country for the right people. But we had to convince our financial partners of this fact. We believed they came on board because we put a powerful business case to them. We convinced them of the book's merits. But, as importantly, *we convinced them of why the book would help their cause.*

And that's the ultimate leadership secret of successful entrepreneurs: They have the ability to get people to want to work with them or buy from them because their business gives people what they truly want. So as you think about starting your own business or improving your business, think about how you can tap into other people's self interest. If you really want to achieve what you want to achieve, help others achieve what they want to achieve. Think in terms of "We" not "Me".

They'll only dare if you really demonstrate you care: How to be a Model Mentor:

"Mentor: a loyal advisor of Odysseus entrusted with the care and education of Telemachus; a wise and trusted counselor"
Webster's Dictionary

In the great Greek myth of The Odyssey, the hero is a man called Odysseus who has to undergo great trials and suffering. However, his life is made easier by his friend and advisor, Mentor, whom he trusts with everything, including the care and education of his son, Telemachus.

And that's where the term, Mentor, comes from. So in order to be a good mentor to someone, you have to be both their friend and trusted advisor. In fact, the trust level has to be so great that the other person would entrust you with the care and education of their children. Makes you think, hey?

So, how good a mentor are you to the people around you? Do they turn to you for inspiration, education, support and empowerment? Do they truly believe that you have their best interests at heart? Do you go out of your way to demonstrate how much you care? You see, your people will only dare to try new things if they know you really care about their well being. And there are so few managers who really care about developing the potential of their people. You know why? Because they are only concerned about their own careers and their own interests. They regard the people around them as nothing more than mere means to an end. You know the joke: To err is human, to forgive is ....not company policy. Seriously, we go into so many companies where the mission statement encourages people to take risks. Then, when they take a risk and fail, they get an AAK - an Attitude Adjustment Klap. And they never take another risk again.

However, there's one core leadership principle that we've discovered: *People who actively demonstrate how much they care about developing their people's potential deliver the best results - in the short term as well as the long term.* So ask yourself how you can help grow your people: Is it through subsidizing their ongoing education? Or is it by being supportive through on-the-job training? Or is it by encouraging lively debate and a culture of challenge and curiosity? Or is it by helping them lead a better quality of life overall through lifestyle education?

And by the way, being a good mentor doesn't stop in the workplace. It means being a friend and trusted advisor to your family as well. The one thing that we've both learnt as entrepreneurs is that there is no dividing line between your business and your family. The two worlds merge. And unless you become a coach and mentor in the workplace, you'll become a tyrant on the homefront as well. We have met so many entrepreneurs whose businesses may have thrived but whose family lives were broken. Simply because they became dictators not developers of people.

Build your network: Be a Go-Giver not a Go-Getter

"He who has saved one life has, as it were, saved the world entire"

Schindlers List

In almost all the motivational literature on offer, readers are encouraged to become Go-Getters - to go out there and grab all they can as fast as they can. We are advising you to become a Go-Giver – someone who always gives more than they take.

We are not telling you to give all you can because we want you to become a charity. We are telling you to give generously because one of the most valuable attributes of any entrepreneur is an extensive, close-knit network of associates. No matter how successful you become, you will always need allies to help you out of a difficult situation. Or you will need partners to help you exploit a specific opportunity. Or you will need people to vouch for you to prospects or clients. Or you will simply need a favour.

There is an ancient African saying that says "A person is a person because of other people." Start building your network now. Do as many favours for other people as you can. Deposit as much as you can into the Relationship Account. We promise you that there will come a time when you will need other people's help. And nothing will destroy you faster than building a reputation as someone who keeps on taking without giving back.

What's more, giving to other people can be a massive pleasure for its own sake. Both of us donate big chunks of our time to charity and helping emerging entrepreneurs. We do it because we know we have to. But we also do it because it gives meaning to our lives. As part of our commitment to helping people grow, we will be giving away hundreds of this book to people who cannot to buy it. If just one person becomes a successful entrepreneur as a result of this gesture, it will have been worth it.

So ask yourself how your business can add value to the community. Look for ways to become a net-contributor to your society. We promise you that whatever you give away will be repaid to you tenfold.

The Secret to maximizing your potential is child's play: Don't get frustrated, get fascinated!!

Frustrate: To make plans or efforts worthless or of no avail; defeat; baffle; nullify

Fascinate: To attract and hold spellbound by a unique power; to arouse the interest or curiosity; to cast under a spell; to capture the interest.

Webster's Dictionary

Here's a tip for all aspiring entrepreneurs: If you want to become more successful, spend more time with children under the age of six. You know why? Because young kids don't get frustrated, they stay fascinated. They are always exploring. They get excited all the time. Everything is an adventure for them. And they ask the most amazing questions. In fact, after you've read this book, read a book called "Children's letters to God". This is a book of illustrated letters that children have written to God. Here is a sample of some of them:

Dear God, why don't you leave the sun out at night because that's when we need it most.

Dear God, you should only let very good friends get married because the neighbours fight all the time.

Dear God, do plastic flowers make you mad? They'd make me mad if I made the real ones.

Dear God, are you rich or just famous?

Dear God, I read your book. Where do you get your ideas?

In fact, if you want to stay successful, we believe some part of you needs to stay a child. Unless you can sustain a childlike fascination for what you're doing, eventually the pressure and the stress will grind down your spirit. We believe it's this childlike idealism and capacity for enthusiasm that sustains many of the country's top entrepreneurs in times of crisis.

So from now on, eliminate the word - "frustrated" - from your vocabulary. And replace it with the word - "fascinated". C'mon, try it.

See the difference it makes. Everytime you come up against a seemingly insurmountable obstacle, say, "This is so fascinating. I wonder how I'm going to get around this." Remember the power of words - they are the labels you attach to your experience. So what would you rather have? A frustrating experience or a fascinating experience?

It's your call.

Love Of The Game:
How to radiate your enthusiasm to motivate others especially in tough times

"What I do best is share my enthusiasm"   *Bill Gates*

The amazing story of St George and the Dragon

The story you're about to read is over 500 years old. But it is as relevant today as it was in the 15th century:

Once upon a time in a land far, far away, there was a king of a magical country. And this king had a beautiful daughter whom he lived very much. So you can imagine his grief and alarm when he awoke one morning to discover that the Dragon had kidnapped his daughter. He knew it was the Dragon because it left its spoor.

The King called all his knights together and declared, "Who ever brings back my daughter from the evil Dragon shall have her hand in marriage and shall be heir to my kingdom!" Now the knights became extremely excited because they all wanted fame, glory, power and status.

Before we continue this story, dear reader and entrepreneur, let us ask you this question: how many times have you become extremely excited about a possibility or project? But then, as the going got tough, drawn out and boring, you lost your desire? Back to the story:

One by one the knights mounted their horses and set out to rescue the princess. They tracked the Dragon for days, weeks, months. Then, they began to give up. Many of the knights declared that the Dragon could not be found. They convinced themselves and their peers that the princess was dead and the quest to save her was a hopeless one. But St George knew there was no such thing as a hopeless situation, only people who become hopeless about a situation. What's more, he truly loved the princess and he was determined to save her. With every step, his resolve strengthened. He felt her fear as she lay in some cave, imprisoned by the Dragon. He cared more about her than about himself. He was the ultimate caring warrior. Eventually, every knight gave up and turned back, except for St George.

Before we continue, dear reader, why do you think St George was the only knight to carry on with his quest? Well, maybe it was his mental toughness; maybe it was his guts and determination. Or maybe it was just his faith. We believe, however, it was because he was doing it for the love while everyone else was just doing it for the money, recognition and power.

Back to the story:

St George carried on alone, motivated by a knowledge deep down inside that the Princess was alive and that he was getting close to his destination. Then, St George saw fresh Dragon spoor, and he knew he was almost there. After a few more kilometres, he discovered the cave where the Dragon kept the princess. He got so close he could hear the Dragon breathing and he could smell the scent of the princess. He unsheathed his sword and he hesitated, unable to go into the cave...

Before we continue, dear reader, why do you think St George hesitated? Why was he unable to enter the cave? What stood between St George and the princess? You may answer that he was scared of the dragon. We agree. But where was the dragon? Not in the cave. In his heart and mind. He had to slay the dragon within before he moved forward. And what could motivate him to slay his inner dragon? Only one thing - his passion and love for the princess. Unless your passion is greater than your fear, your fear will cripple you. Think about it: there's really no difference between you and St George. Only times, places and names have changed. Let's continue with the final part of the story:

St George focused on the princess. He thought about how far he had come. He thought about how he would feel if he turned back. And he knew he couldn't live with himself if he didn't slay his Dragon. So slowly, cautiously, stealthily, he entered the cave. He saw the dragon. Before it could respond, he drove his sword through its heart and killed it instantly. Then he turned to embrace the princess and carry her home to become his bride. And, as the story goes, they both lived happily ever after.

So what are the ultimate lessons of this story:

You have to have a passion for what you're about to do. And whatever you do, you have to do it with passion.

You have to focus on your love for what you're doing when you are faced with massive problems.

Even when others say it can't be done, go with your own gut feel.

Just before you launch your own business or achieve massive success, you will be faced with your biggest challenge.

Whatever happens, don't turn back when you're almost there.

If you do it for the love, the rest will follow.

If you just do it for the money, you will fail.

Be an Amateur, not a Professional

Often, in Mike's talks, he tells the audience that he's not doing it for the money. They all laugh at him and shake their heads in disbelief. Mike then tells them that he's going to take their money but he's not doing it for the money. They laugh even louder but they nod their heads in understanding.

We promise you that when all is said and done, the ultimate ingredient for success is the sheer love of the game - especially when the game isn't going your way. You see, it's one thing to love the business when you're winning. It's quite another thing to love the business when the business isn't going well. In fact, it's your love of the game that will get you through your defeats. And that's one of the main differences between those who make it and those who don't: *The winners never lose their love and passion for what they're doing.*

So here's a little tip: Print some posters that boldly declare the following five words:

Yes! I Love This Business!

Stick these posters up wherever you are most likely to see them everyday. Make sure your people see these posters. And make sure your customers see these posters. These five words must become a constant reminder of why you're doing what you're doing and how you should behave each and every day.

You see, the moment you question whether you really should have done what you've done, you lose your personal power. You know why? Because self-doubt creeps into your spirit. Instead of concentrating all your energy on doing what you do excellently, you focus your energy on whether you made the right decision or not to go into the business. And the moment that happens, your passion evaporates like mist before the rising sun.

Now look, we're aren't telling you to be stupid here. There may come a time when you decide you need to get out the business. And if that time comes, make your decision. But, up front, commit yourself to giving it all you have for a certain period - maybe it's two years or maybe it's three. But there are too many would-be entrepreneurs who fail because they don't give their passion a chance.

Never forget that it's a game – a big game, but still a game:

How do you feel when you say to yourself, "I have to work!"?

Now, how do you feel when you say to yourself, "Time to play!"

Can you feel the difference? Well, just as an athlete plays a game or an actor plays a role, you are playing the game called, "My Own Business".

And you know what? Your game is the most exciting game of all. We promise you that if you are the kind of person who has bought this book and made it this far, you are the kind of person who is going to win their game.

As two entrepreneurs who have been running our own businesses for over seven years, we can tell you that once you succeed at the game called "My Own Business", you never want to stop playing. The worst day in the game called "Your Own Business", is better than the most ecstatic day working for someone else. But when we are tired, scared, or frustrated, we still have to keep reminding ourselves that this is a game. And thank God, we're still playing it.

There is nothing more common than entrepreneurs who've "made it" in the short term only to lose it all very shortly thereafter. The secret to sustained success lies in continually focusing on the magic of being your own boss. When the chips are down, when the market is tight, when the budget is not being met, when the cashflow is being squeezed, when the bank manager threatens you, when customers return goods, when you can't meet orders because you're out of stock, when your people don't perform or when the weather turns against you, that's when you have to remember that it's a game you love to play. You have to remember that any game, no matter how exhilarating, needs to be lost sometimes. Otherwise it's not a game, it's just make-believe.

The Pleasure-Pain Exercise

Here's an interesting exercise for you to truly decide whether you love the entrepreneur game you're about to go into, or the one you're already in: Take a piece of paper and draw a line down the middle, dividing the paper in half. Now think about all the highly pleasurable reasons why you're going solo. C'mon, think about all the elements that have motivated you to take the ultimate leap. And write them all down on the right side of the paper. Spend time on this exercise and think about every last thing.

Now think about all the potential negative reasons why you shouldn't play the entrepreneurial game. Think about all the sources of pain that come with the game. Write them all down on the left-hand side of the paper. Write down everything.

Now look at the two lists. Does the list on the right far outstrip the list on the left? If it doesn't, it could mean one of three things: Either you need to change your attitude towards the business and remind yourself why you love it so much, or you need to change your strategy in the way you are managing the business, or you need to get the hell out as soon as possible.

By the way, we did this exercise and this is what we came up with:

Pain	Pleasure
Fear	Freedom
Anxiety	Pride
Frustration	Honour
Loss	Victory
Rejection	Recognition
Fatigue	Glory
Embarrassment	Growth
Loneliness	Fulfillment
	Thrill
	Adventure
	Excitement
	Contribution
	Self-esteem
	Independence
	Making a difference
	Adrenaline
	Leadership
	Wealth
	Pioneering
	Fun

How competitive are you?
How powerful is your desire to win?

If "Your Own Business" is a game, you have to play the game against somebody. And unless you're ESKOM, you're going to have competition. And your competition is going to be good and it's going to keep getting better. So how competitive are you? How powerful is your desire to win?

Vince Lombardi, the famous coach of the American Football team - the Greenbay Packers, said it well:

"Winning is not a sometime thing; it's an all-the-time thing. You don't win once in a while, you don't do things right once in a while, you do them right all the time. Winning is a habit. Unfortunately, so is losing...
I don't care what people say about me as long as I win. I don't give a damn about the statistics as long as I win. Winning is like a drug. It's a hard thing to kick.

Second place is meaningless. You can't always be first, but you have to believe that you should have been - that you are never beaten, time just runs out on you".

Winning the game of "Your Own Business" means that you have to constantly track the competition, know what they're doing, do what they do better, and beat them to the customer. At the same time, winning this game means not being reactive to the competition. It means constantly leading the competition and doing things they haven't even dreamed of doing.

You want to know the truth? One of the main reasons why we are writing this book is to leave our competition in the dust. This kind of book, combining insight on motivation, business management and franchising, has never been published before. It is a win for us. We've redefined the game.

For this moment, we're in the lead. But the lead could change tomorrow. That's just the way it is. So we will keep competing. We will keep winning. There may come a time when the competition passes us. But it won't be for long. You know why? Because we love to compete. We love to win. And we love this business!!

It's not good enough being a leader, you have to be a cheerleader. Become famous for your enthusiasm.

Know this truth: the moment you start your own business, you become a source of energy to everyone around you. Depending on your behaviour, you either become a positive source of energy or a negative one. We promise you that if you come to work in a bad mood, you will infect everyone around you with it. That day, the productivity of your business will suffer. You will lose business you could have won if you acted like you were excited.

If you want to become a highly successful entrepreneur, it's not good enough just being a leader - you have to be a cheerleader. You cannot afford to walk around like a bear with a sore paw. You cannot afford to indulge in your own self-pity parties. You cannot afford to give in to your disappointments or frustrations. You know why? Because your every move, word and gesture is being scrutinized by those around you.

If you think that you're going through stress, multiply that stress by ten and you may get close to the stress that your people will be going through. At least you're in control. At least you have the massive dream to sustain you. At least, you have the future income to look forward to. But your people at the rockface are dependent almost entirely on you. The chances are that they are surviving on a very tight budget. They are worried about the future. Their morale levels fluctuate from day to day. They tend to focus on the negative because that's the natural tendency of many people.

What are we saying? Simply this: If you show that you cannot handle the stress, or if you demonstrate your anxiety, your people's morale will crumble like a puff pastry. When you are in front of people who depend on you for a living, you have to demonstrate how confident you are in the future. You have to transmit your faith and optimism at every opportunity.

In fact, you have to make a superhuman effort to motivate people constantly. People have three basic needs: *Security, Recognition and Love*. And whether you like it or not, you have to give them all three. If you choose your people carefully, they will work damn hard with you to get the business up and running. But good people are high maintenance people. They require a lot of TLC - tender loving care.

They need you to pick them up, pat them on the back and hug them every now and then. This function is as important a contributor to your success as anything else you do in your business.

We know what you're thinking. Some of you may not be natural expressives or extroverts. It doesn't matter. You have to do whatever you have to do in your own personal style. You have to find a way that's comfortable for you but you have to find a way. We make you this promise: *Neglect the emotions of your people, and your business will perish.*

And by the way, in the age of the internet and outsourcing, we aren't just speaking about the people who work directly for you. We're talking about all the "virtual partners" you will have. These are all the service and product providers who will help you in your business.

So are you a Walking Rallying Cry or are you the Walking Wounded? When you are with colleagues or customers, do you lift them up or do you bring them down? Think about it - because your business will thrive if you lead by example. And your business will die if you don't.

Become famous for your enthusiasm. Be the kind of person who others want to join because your spirit is so buoyant. In South Africa right now, people are being overwhelmed with problems and stress. They will flock to anyone who can light them up with hope and joy in times of darkness. And you know what? It doesn't matter whether you are selling coffee or construction, customers are attracted to the light. So shine yours brightly.

And by the way, did you know that the word "enthusiasm" comes from the Greek word, Entheos, which means Godlike. Makes you think, doesn't it?

Sometimes, you have to be a clown

"I don't want to become too serious. I'm considered the clown of the team, because I cannot be serious for two minutes. I'm afraid if I become more serious, I will stop winning" **Alberto Tomba - Two Time Olympic Gold Medallist**

Sometimes, it pays to be a clown. It pays to do things that make your people and your customers laugh. Remember the power of the Court Jester: In the middle ages, the jester was the second most powerful person in the kingdom after the king because he made people laugh while he was telling the truth. If you truly want to capture the attention of others, make sure you amuse and entertain them. But do it in a way that is respectful and appropriate.

This point is especially appropriate to those people who have a great sense of humour. If you have this skill, use it to maximum. If you haven't, try to develop it. But don't force it.

And by the way, have you noticed how we always seem to be able to laugh at misfortune after the event. We look back at the incident and smile. Our question to you is: Why wait? Laugh about it now!

The marketplace is not a charity organization: you have to be strong for others

The marketplace is not the SPCA, it's not the YMCA and it's not the Red Cross. The marketplace doesn't care about your personal problems. It doesn't care about your marital hassles, your overdraft or your losses on the stock exchange. Your customers and employees don't care about your problems, they expect you to solve their problems.

So here's an important rule in the game called Success: *Don't burden others with your troubles. Don't moan about how tough things are. Don't give your customers excuses why you didn't meet your promises.* They don't care and, what's more, your excuses will only make them angry.

We meet so many mediocre operators who are continually complaining about how tough their life is. The moment we hear the complaints start, we know this operator will never get into The High Performance Zone. Mentally, we shut down and we look for somebody who is rising to the challenge with guts and enthusiasm.

If you are going to succeed, you need to play a number of roles. You are not just an entrepreneur, you are a social worker, a psychologist, a marriage counselor, a big brother or sister, a best friend or soulmate, a father confessor, a shoulder to cry on or just someone to lean on when your associates are not strong.

In other words, you have to be a social chameleon. You have to play whatever role the situation calls for. Some roles will come easier to you than others. But just because playing a certain role doesn't come easily to you, it doesn't mean you can afford not to play it. Obviously, there may be times when you have to call in a professional but remember the triple A's of the entrepreneur: Adapt, Adjust, Advance.

Surround yourself with people who will recharge your batteries

Being an entrepreneur is an emotionally, intellectually and physically exhausting existence. You have to keep giving to the people around you without expecting the favour to be returned. However, you are human. We are human. We all need someone to help us help others.

So here's our advice: surround yourself with a handful of people who will recharge your batteries. These are the people with whom you can share your real problems. These are the people who love you just the way you are. They don't judge you. They have your best interests at heart. They love to help you because it gives them pleasure.

If you're really lucky, you have a spouse that can also play this role with you. Or you may already have a few very good friends who will be there for you. However, we recommend that you expand this group. Search out the best of the best and connect with them. Establish your own personal board of directors. And, most importantly, ensure that you always give the people around you more than you take from them.

And that's one of the reasons, we wrote this book *together*. We both have separate strengths. We both could have written separate books. But we decided to pool our talents and fire off each other's energy and ideas. This book isn't Eric's way and it's not Mike's way, it's a higher way paved with the synergy of two champions playing together.

Being an entrepreneur is a paradox. On the one hand, you have to fly solo. You are on your own, taking leaps of faith without a safety net. It's a lonely existence because you are the boss. You have to make the decisions. You have to lead others. You are responsible. You are accountable.

On the other hand, you need the cross-pollination of other people's ideas. You need the inspiration and insight of quality people from inside your industry and out. You need the moral support of likeminded champions facing similar challenges. In other words, you need to create a web of human resources that you can draw on when you need it most. So right now, begin contacting the people you want to align yourself with, attend industry functions where you can meet the people you need. Decide what you're going to give to others as part of the "talent trade".

Finally, Find the Applause Within

At the end of 1997, Mike attended a marvelous program at the Disney University in Orlando, Florida. The program was called "The Disney Approach to People Management" and it lasted three days. During this program, Mike was exposed to how Disney runs its theme parks and achieves such high levels of customer delight.

At one of the workshops, the facilitator told the delegates that at Disney, the real heroes of customer service "find the applause within". In other words, they don't need other people to tell them how good they are for them to feel good about themselves. They are constantly praising themselves and celebrating their own victories and successes.

So here's our point: take time to congratulate yourself; Become your own biggest fan; Celebrate all your successes, no matter how small; Give yourself credit when credit is due; and forgive yourself immediately for mistakes.

Here are five unquestionable truths of an entrepreneur:

If you don't praise yourself, you'll end up praising no-one.

If you don't forgive yourself, you'll end up forgiving no-one.

If you don't love what you see in the mirror, you'll end up loving no-one.

If you don't say nice things to yourself, you'll end up saying nothing nice to anyone.

If you're not comfortable with yourself, you'll end up being uncomfortable with everyone.

The Power of Self-Awareness:
How to use the Power of Conscious Thinking to achieve the results you desire.

"Self observation brings man to the realization of the necessity of self-change. And in observing himself, a man notices that self-observation itself brings about certain changes in his inner processes. He begins to understand that self-observation is an instrument of self-change, a means of awakening."
George Gurdjieff

If there is one factor that sets man apart from other animals, it's the ability to choose. Birds operate on a genetic code embedded deep within their brains. Mammals operate on instinct and conditioning. Only humans have the gift of conscience and consciousness. The problem, though, like all other gifts, is that we may have the gift but we don't use the gift. And so the gift loses its power. In this session we will show you how to leverage the gift of Self-Awareness. We will demonstrate the Power of Choice and Conscious Thinking. And finally we will show you how to help others do the same.

A Personal Self-Awareness Test
Here's a Self-Awareness test for you to take before we continue with this session:

Rate yourself out of ten for each attribute:

1. I never lose my temper with other people   _____
2. When times are tough, others turn to me for support   _____
3. I keep my head when others are losing theirs   _____
4. I take nothing for granted   _____
5. I am extremely sensitive to the feelings of others   _____
6. I am continually talking positively to myself   _____
7. I am continually aware of my emotions   _____

8. Even when I'm tired, I'm aware of my impact on others _____
9. I consciously seek change and new challenges   _____
10. I'm always evaluating my actions and looking for ways
    to improve myself   _____

                                          TOTAL _____

If you scored 85+, you are a master practitioner of the Power of Self-Awareness. This session will merely fine-tune your skills.

If you scored 74-85, you are very good at Self-Awareness and this session will help you take yourself to the next level.

If you scored less than 74, this session will give you an edge that will prove invaluable to you.

The wristwatch exercise

Do this exercise right now: take your wristwatch off your left wrist and place it on your right wrist. Do it now. We promise you that for the next 4-6 weeks you will continually look at your left wrist for the time even though the watch is on your right wrist. Why? Habit and conditioning. If you wear your watch on your left wrist, your brain has been conditioned to refer to your left wrist for the time. It will take 4-6 weeks to "re-condition" your brain to refer to your right wrist. (This information, by the way, is based on personal research completed by Mike on himself.)

Now, if it takes your brain 4-6 weeks simply to re-condition itself for this simple task, imagine how much more challenging it is to change other more complex, deep rooted habits. But that's exactly what this session is all about. It's about consciously "rewiring" your mind to respond to situations in the most effective manner, not in the manner that you've become used to doing.

The trademark of highly successful entrepreneurs:
They are always seeking change and new ways to ignite their businesses.

You see, the reason why we form habits is that it allows the brain to focus on new challenges. If we had to relearn everything everyday, obviously we couldn't function. However, there are certain aspects of our lives that we need to unlearn. There are certain habits that we need to get rid of. There are certain habits we need to acquire.

There is knowledge we need to learn.

All of these challenges mean that our brains are in a constant state of change. It means that there always has to be a degree of discomfort as the brain adjusts to new realities. However, the difference between those who succeed and those don't is very often the way they're able to live with this discomfort. Those people who keep seeking the Comfort Zone and avoid change will fail. While those who consciously seek the High Performance Zone and romance change will thrive.

Like anything else, programming your brain for change is an acquired skill. The more time you invest in this skill, the better you will be. And that's another reason why we are writing this book. It's a brand new, hugely challenging experience for both of us. We know that this book will make us both more effective entrepreneurs because we are exercising mental muscles that we may never have used before.

And that's the trademark of highly successful entrepreneurs: They are always seeking change and new ways to ignite their businesses. Almost every moment of every day, they are searching for the next breakthrough idea that will sustain their success. Their minds are in perpetual motion: seeking, seeking, seeking. Is yours? We have to believe it is otherwise you would not have made it this far.

Switch off your automatic pilot and switch on your mental radar

In his classic novel, The Great Gatsby, Scott Fitzgerald described Jay Gatsby as a man "with a heightened sensitivity to the promises of life". We believe he was describing a key attribute of great entrepreneurs. They are hyper sensitive to the opportunities and possibilities around them. They see openings and prospects where others see nothing. They have trained themselves to take nothing for granted. They filter everything through their "opportunity radar".

That's why we don't believe successful entrepreneurs are "lucky". The Webster's Dictionary defines luck as "success that is the result of chance". If anything, successful entrepreneurs make their own luck. Because they are always consciously exploring new territory, they are always discovering new opportunities.

So, from this moment on, switch off your automatic pilot. Take nothing for granted. Look for the opportunity behind everything. Switch on your mental radar. You'll be amazed at how much you'll see if you consciously look for what's hidden to the unconscious eye. So here's a little exercise:

Think about three typical aspects of your business that are considered established ways of operating. Now think about how you can change each of these aspects to deliver better results. So for example in our case, we looked at this book and said:

1. 99% of books are distributed through publishers. But why don't we do it ourselves?
2. There are books on motivation. And there are books on starting your own business. Why don't we combine the two and add a vital chapter on Franchising and franchises?
3. It's very difficult to effectively market a book in South Africa because of lack of funds. So why don't we find sponsors to help us?

T.S. Eliot, the great British poet, said it well when he wrote:
We shall not cease from exploration,
And the end of all our exploring,
Will be to arrive where we started
And know the place for the first time.
What are we saying to you? Simply this: Keep seeing old things with fresh eyes. Inspiration and excellence are all around you, all you have to do is look for them.

Use your MCTV: Be aware of your conduct at all times

Your MCTV is your Mental Circuit Television. Let us ask you, how many times have you said something to someone and then immediately regretted what you've said? How many times have you unconsciously showed your irritation or tiredness to someone and then regretted it? How many times has someone told you their name and then you immediately forgot it? How many times have you seen two people talk to each other but not really communicate because they were not aware of their impact on the other person? How many times have you wished that you could go back and do something over because you just didn't give it all you had first time around?

You see, unless we are constantly aware of our own conduct, we cannot consistently perform at our peak. The mark of a true champion is their ability to evaluate what they are doing while they are doing it in the context of what's going on around them. That's what makes a great leader. Their ability to act, think and anticipate at the same time.

So from now on, run your own MCTV. When you are with others observe yourself talking to them. Pretend there's a little video monitor in your skull. Watch the impact you have on others. Then adjust your behaviour accordingly. Ask yourself whether, if you were the other person, you would enjoy listening to you. See things from the point of view of others. Walk in their shoes. Feel with their hearts. And take action.

Practice this technique today. Practice it tomorrow. Keep asking yourself whether you are a force for excitement and possibility – especially when you're tired. It's easy to be outstanding and self-aware when you're fresh. It's quite another story when you're at the edge of your resources. That's when the leaders separate themselves from the pack.

So here's a little tip to help you with your MCTV. Write the phrase, "My MCTV is making me sharper everyday" wherever you are likely to see it. Write it in your diary, on your bathroom mirror, on your rearview mirror, on your screensaver. Keep reminding yourself over and over again. Repetition is the mother of learning. So keep yourself under constant surveillance.

Here's a "self-surveillance" exercise for you to do right now: Think carefully about the three most self-destructive habits you want to change. And then think about three self-constructive habits you want to acquire. Consciously go about this mission. Once you've made these changes, identify another set of habits and continue with the process neverendingly.

How to exercise the Power of Choice: pause, evaluate, decide, act, be slow to anger, be quick to forgive

Many would-be entrepreneurs fail even though they have the ability, the resources and the passion. You know why? Because they dare where angels fear to tread. They fire before knowing where they're even aiming. They become victims of their passion and temper. They allow their hearts to rule their heads.

Being a highly successful entrepreneur is a high-wire balancing act. On the one hand you have to be able to pause and coolly evaluate a situation. On the other hand, you must be decisive. On the one hand you must be passionate about what you're doing. On the other hand, you can't afford to take it too seriously. On the one hand, you must rarely lose your temper. On the other hand, you must always forgive. On the one hand, you must trust others. On the other, you must be extremely vigilant.

So, in order to be a great entrepreneur, you have to be mildly schizophrenic. Albert Einstein summed it up well when he said, "The true mark of a genius is the ability to hold two conflicting thoughts in your mind at the same time and still function."

The Seven Vital Self-Awareness Questions

By definition, if you're an entrepreneur, you're going to be someone who influences, persuades and leads others. Entrepreneurs are agents of change. They're out there in front where others are too afraid to go. So like it or not, if you're going to be an entrepreneur, you're going to be a role model to others. They're going to look to you for answers, for hope and for guidance. In order for you to fulfill that function you need to answer the Seven Vital Self-Awareness Questions especially in times of crisis. Here they are:

1. Am I at my best when things are at their worst?
2. What's great about this situation?
3. What am I noticing in this situation?
4. What am I learning from this situation?
5. What will I do differently in the future?
6. Am I being a role model to others through my conduct in this situation?
7. Am I making myself proud by doing the right thing in this situation?

Here's an amusing story of how Mike answered the Seven Self-Awareness Questions in a recent personal experience:

"I was conducting a seminar in the city of East London. I arrived the night before and stayed at the King David Hotel on Curry Street.

When I got back to my car the following morning, I noticed that the rear right window had been broken. On closer inspection, I also noticed that the radio had been stolen as well as a box of 400 audiocassettes that I left on the back seat of the car. As I sold these cassettes for R60 each and I was uninsured, I had just lost close to R24000."

Before we continue, dear reader, think about how you would feel in this situation. C'mon, put yourself in Mike's shoes. What would be going through your mind right now? Back to the story

" Well, I just couldn't believe it. I became incredibly angry. I wanted to scream in utter frustration. Then I started to feel sorry for myself. I asked the fatal question, "Why does this have to happen to me?" I began to get upset and demotivated. The more I thought about the theft, the worse my mental state became. I became especially anxious because I knew that in just one hour I would have to motivate almost 500 people. I just didn't feel like doing it now. All I could think about was how much money I had lost and how unfair life was."

Dear reader, can you identify with Mike's feelings? Have you ever been in a similar situation? What would you do next? Back to the story

"Then I interrupted my negative thought pattern. I knew I had to turn my attitude around before the seminar otherwise things would go from bad to worse. I knew I had to walk my talk. So I asked myself whether I was being my best during a bad time. The answer was no. So I resolved to quit feeling sorry for myself. After all, I had left the box on the back seat of the car. I had to take responsibility.

"Then I asked myself, what was great about the situation. At first, my brain shouted "nothing!!" But I kept asking the question until my brain said to me, "As a result of this theft, you have just motivated 400 youths in the city of East London. Secondly, you have involuntarily made a contribution to GEAR and the RDP. Thirdly, you have started a thriving trade in motivational cassettes. Fourthly, as a result of listening to your tapes, the people who stole them will give up crime!" Before I knew it, I was feeling a lot more motivated. Which just goes to show: if you ask the right questions, you get the right answers.

"Then I asked myself what I was noticing in the situation. I realized that I was focusing only on the negative of the stolen cassettes. I switched focus to the fact that 500 people had paid to come and hear me speak. That was a massive privilege. It was also a huge reason to be ecstatic not depressed.

"Then I asked myself what I learnt from the situation. The answer was simple: firstly, never to leave valuable possessions on the back seat of a car at night. Secondly, to stay focused on the magic not the tragic. And thirdly, to consciously make the choice to be happy in any situation.

"Then I asked myself what I would do differently in the future. Again the answer was simple: firstly to lock my things away. Secondly, to obey my instincts and not be lazy. The night before, I had looked at the box and wondered whether I should take it into the hotel for safekeeping. I knew I should, but I decided not to because the car was parked in a fenced off, guarded area.

"I also knew I was being a role model to others in this situation because I had converted it from a catastrophe to a valuable learning experience and story. I knew I would make myself proud by using misfortune to make me stronger and to help others do the same.

"Finally, I used the story to start off the seminar and the audience loved it. I made them laugh while they recalled similar experiences. I would never have been able to illustrate my points so clearly if the theft had never happened."

So from today, keep the Seven Vital Self-Awareness Questions close to you - especially during times of crisis. They will direct your brain to help you resolve even the toughest challenges.

A separate, vital family question:
Am I being a hero to my kids?

In 1998, MTN gave Mike a sponsorship to motivate matric students throughout South Africa. Mike went into schools and spent time with the students. He asked them what their biggest source of stress was. Guess what their response was? Their parents. Not exams, not the future, not the jobmarket, their parents. Many of the kids told Mike that their fathers and mothers were suffering from extreme stress.

They said that their houses were places of tension and uncertainty. And this home strife was affecting their academic performance.

So here's the challenge facing entrepreneurs: you have to manage the stress of being your own boss while facilitating an environment of love, support and togetherness at home. You have to be a hero to your kids while you take on the world at work. After all, aren't your kids a major reason why you're doing it anyway?

Here's the ultimate Great Daddy or Mommy Test: Do your kids want to be like you when they grow up? Do they look at you and see an outstanding future? Do they look at you and see a victim or a victor? Do you represent hope and optimism?

Listen to your emotions – they're trying to tell you something

As an entrepreneur, we can promise you one thing with total certainty: you will go on an emotional rollercoaster ride. You will experience joy, pain, frustration, disappointment, fulfillment, overload, confusion and rejection - sometimes all in a single day.

The best entrepreneurs are aware of their emotions and they understand what their emotions are telling them. Here are the signals your most powerful emotions are sending you:

Fear: Get prepared and be alert. You're about to go where you've never gone before. Use your fear to make you sharp.
Anger: You may be going through a tough time and you're taking it out on others. They may not even be aware they have done something to annoy you. Understand why they did it. Forgive them. Move on.
Frustration: You are using a strategy that isn't working. Change it or give it time.
Overload: You've got a lot on your plate. Chunk down and focus on the most important thing you have to do. The rest will take care of itself.
Disappointment: Something that you expected to happen is not going to happen. Change your expectations. Don't dwell on missed opportunities, concentrate on new possibilities.
Rejection: Someone didn't buy your product or respond favourably to you. It's probably got nothing even to do with you. Don't take it

personally. Don't let the worst part of someone else control the best part of you.

Inadequacy: You either need to change the way you look at the situation or you need to get the skills to deal with the situation. Most often, you simply need to believe in yourself more fully.

Uncertainty and doubt: Have faith that you will make it and be successful. Ask your Higher Power for help.

Consciously go for the Eight Positive Emotions of Power

Love: Love your fellow human beings and love what you're doing.

Confidence: Know that you can deal with anything that arises. Back yourself to the hilt.

Gratitude: Thank your Higher Power for your gifts and your personal power.

Excitement: Rev up your engine by focusing on why you're so passionate about what you're doing.

Humility: Be aware of the wonder of life and the magic around you.

Contribution: Keep asking how you can give to the people around you. Practice interdependence.

Vitality: Stay healthy through proper eating and exercise. Your body is your machine. It's your temple. Treat it accordingly.

Flexibility: Keep adapting to your environment. If something isn't working, change it.

Finally, get feedback – the breakfast of champions

To conclude this session, we have one final call to action for you: Get feedback from the people who matter. And don't be afraid of criticism. Don't shoot the messenger. Consciously encourage and reward your staff and customers for telling you what they think.

The Power to Endure

How to develop the persistence of the Cheetah: Learn to love those setbacks; Stay focused when you're tired; Keep foraging for the business

Persistence: To continue steadily or firmly in some purpose or course of action, especially in spite of opposition; to stand firm; to last or endure.

Webster's Dictionary

The Ten Point Persistence Test

Before you start this session, put yourself through the Ten Point Persistence Test. On a scale of 1-10, score yourself on each attribute:

1. I love a big challenge _____
2. I never, ever give up _____
3. When I make a mistake, I recover immediately _____
4. No matter how many setbacks I experience, I always expect to succeed _____
5. I perform really well at the end of the day _____
6. I love being my own boss _____
7. I want to help other people _____
8. I don't allow others to pull me down _____
9. Everything that happens to me, teaches me
10. I am indestructible _____

Total _____

Scores

If you scored 85+, you already have the persistence of a cheetah. This session will merely reinforce your formidable spirit.

If you scored 70-84, You're the persevering type. This session will help strengthen your mental muscle and bolster your resilience.

If you scored less than 70, it's time to start training. This session will toughen you up and help you get ready to go out hunting as an entrepreneur.

A cheetah never feels "rejected" because it misses its prey

We have chosen the Cheetah as our role model for entrepreneurs. Do you know why? Because despite its hunting prowess, speed and predatory gifts, the cheetah misses its prey nine out of ten times. Nine out of ten times!! Can you imagine what would happen to the cheetah if on the ninth time it sat under a tree and exclaimed, "Bugger this, I think I'll become a vegetarian!"

That's why a cheetah will never starve. It may go through lean times. It may go hungry on occasion. It may have to leave its traditional hunting grounds in search of prey. But it knows it has no option: it must continue the hunt - for its sake and the sake of the family it may be sustaining.

A cheetah never feels "rejected" because it misses its prey. It doesn't suffer self-doubt or self-pity. What's more, when it begins its hunt - it always expects to succeed, no matter how many times it doesn't. And that's one of the ultimate secrets of high performance: The best of the breed always expect to win, no matter how many times they don't. We call it pathological optimism - the inability to conceive of defeat even against all odds. You know why? Because the moment you do, you dilute your personal power with FUD - fear, uncertainty and doubt. Think about your own experiences. Think about what happened to your confidence and credibility when you contemplated the consequences of failure and loss. Not pretty memories, are they?

Now look, we aren't telling you to be Pollyanna here. We aren't telling you to be foolhardy and ignorant of the risks you're about to face. You can't walk through your garden shouting "There are no weeds, there are no weeds" and expect the weeds to go away. The weeds will take your garden over. What we are telling you to do is always believe that you can deal with the weeds even if your garden is covered with them. But you better have the right equipment, weedkiller and skills.

Seriously, persistence is directly related to self belief and optimism. Time and time again, we have seen that the most persistent entrepreneurs demonstrate these traits in abundance. In fact, they have developed such a powerful personal mission and attitude that tough times merely strengthen their determination and resilience. It's as though they dare life to throw as much as it can at them so they can hurl it back with interest. If you are feeling a kindred spirit with these champions - welcome to an awesome future as an entrepreneur!!

"I don't focus on the "No", I focus on the R1000 I've just made"

Like the cheetah, Mike misses his prey nine out of ten times. In other words, for every nine "No's" he gets one "Yes". But when he gets a "Yes", he usually makes R10,000. So let's do the arithmetic: if it takes ten calls to make R10,000, each call is worth R1000. That's why he stays so massively persistent in the face of adversity. As Mike says, "I don't focus on the "No", I focus on the R1000 I've just made". Try it out. It works.

Martin Seligman, the author of the book, Learned Optimism, calls it your "Explanatory Style". He states that it is the way we explain things to ourselves that determines our response to those things. If you explain it to yourself negatively, that's how you will respond. If you explain it positively, you will respond accordingly. So start practicing a positive "explanatory style" immediately and enjoy the rewards.

Life is a numbers game

The more times you step up to bat, the more times you will hit the ball for a six. But you have to be prepared to lose a couple wickets along the way. In fact, in the game of life, it doesn't matter how many wickets you lose. What matters is how many times you get back onto the pitch to face another ball.

Let us ask you this question: How many people do you know who have the quality of true persistence? Think about those people who endure against all odds, who roll with the punches and come back stronger than ever, who sustain their spirit in the face of defeat and disappointment. Can you think of any? We guarantee you that these special human beings are the people who make all progress happen. They understand that success is a life game with no time outs. They know that true achievement is the result of thousands of everyday efforts that culminate in victory, glory, wealth, contribution and happiness.

Every single day we hear about people suffering from burnout, depression and stress. We hear about people throwing in the towel. We hear people muttering about the state of the nation and the economy. We hear reasons why it can't be done. We hear stories of impossibility and despair. Well, these are not people in the High Performance Zone. These are not the people who are making it happen. These are not the South African heroes who are edging their way forward inch by inch. These are not the people who have made it this far in this book. These people are not you.

So here's our warning to you: Beware of those who would bring you down. Be vigilant of those who would discourage you from climbing the mountain. They may even mean well. They may even have your interests at heart. But they are not imbued with the spirit of the climber. They live in fear of even trying to explore new territory. Anant Singh, the highly successful film producer and entrepreneur, put it best when he said, "I have faith in my intuition. When I feel that a particular concept has huge potential, I will go with it, despite the doubts and negative feedback of others. I have learnt to have faith in my judgement and not to be infected by the scepticism of others."

The Lobster Principle: Often, people want to pull others down because it makes them feel more significant

Here's a humorous story with a lot of truth: Mike recently conducted a workshop in Saldanha Bay on the West Coast. During a break in the session, he went down to the beach where he saw a fisherman taking a tray of lobsters to the market. However, he was carrying a huge pile of lobsters and the tray was very shallow. Mike could see lobsters climbing over each other as they tried to escape the tray.

Mike shouted to the fisherman, warning him that the lobsters were about to climb out the tray. The fisherman shouted back that they wouldn't. "Why?" asked Mike. "Because", replied the fisherman,

"These are South African lobsters. When one climbs up, ten will pull him back down!!" How true is this story??

So here's our twin message: Firstly, don't let others pull you down in your quest for personal greatness. And secondly, don't try to pull others down. If you do, you're the one that will fall the farthest. Never, ever badmouth your competition. It leaves a sour taste in other people's mouths because they know you could say the same things about them one day.

Love those setbacks: Life can only be lived forwards but it can only be understood backwards

If there's one secret that will keep you consistently motivated and persistent, it's that *there are no setbacks, only valuable experiences.* Time and time again, you will hit roadblocks and dead-ends. You will wonder why you ever decided to start your business. You will experience the worst that life and other people can throw at you. You will come close to the edge. You will hang on by your finger tips. You will scream and you will cry. You will be betrayed and cheated. Your friends will leave you and your enemies will try to get you. Success will elude you. Failure will haunt you.

But you know what? You will endure. You will triumph. You will make it. You will achieve your dream. You know why? Because you understand that whatever happens, it happens for a single, most important reason: to teach you, to grow you, to help you become the champion you dream about now.

Think about all the "setbacks" you've endured until now. Think about what they taught you. Think about the strength you derived from them. Here's the truth: We learn far more from any setback than we do from our victories. So, from now on, don't just endure your setbacks, love them. They've been sent to grow and develop you. We promise you that this attitude of loving your mishaps, missteps and misfires will greatly empower you to achieve your goals.

Think about this: What happens when you curse the people, things and experiences around you? Do you make matters worse? Do you say things that you regret later? Do you stay in the hole longer? Yes, yes and yes!

So try this approach and see what happens: The next time you come face to face with a setback, problem or mishap, look skyward and thank the big entrepreneur in the sky for giving you a learning opportunity. Clench your fist and shout "YES!!". Focus on the fact that you're about to have a breakthrough and then transmit this attitude to others.

We meet so many entrepreneurs who are consumed with anger and anxiety because of the crises that plague them everyday in this crazy country. While they are still making a profit, we can see them beginning to unravel. We can see their resolve weakening. We sense that their commitment is wavering. They're at the beginning of their end.

On the other hand, we have the pleasure of spending time with those entrepreneurs who relish their daily challenges. Like the cheetah, they just keep on foraging for the business. They know that the struggle is its own reward. They know that as long as they're in the game, they're eventually going to win. They know the privilege of freedom is worth any sacrifice. And that's ultimately what this book is all about: How deeply rooted is your desire for emotional and financial independence? If it's deep enough, you will be indestructible. To paraphrase Thami Mazwai, CEO of Mafube Publishing, "You may bend but you will never break".

JOLT – Just-One-Last-Try – because the world is filled with early settlers

Despite everything that we've said in this book so far, there is one thing that really separates the great-ones from the also-rans: The great-ones give it Just-One-Last-Try while the also-rans go home. The great-ones know that the very last call is the call that delivers the results. You know why? Because that's when the competition has given up for the day.

It's the last try that builds the physical and mental muscle. It's the last try that impresses the customer. It's the state of the store or the state of the team at the end of the game that determines ultimate success or failure. It's not how you start but how you finish the game that counts. Put this point to the test: Call on companies between 17h00 and 18h00 during the week. See how they treat you. Go into stores just as they're closing and sample the results. Be the last to leave a restaurant and witness their treatment of you. Just like we have, you will discover that the champions always give it Just-One-Last-Try. They finish like professionals.

You see, the world is full of early settlers. These are the people who stop at the first obstacle and give up. They hit the cul-de-sac and go home. They don't realize that the cul-de-sac isn't the end of the road, it's the beginning of another. That's why this nation's most precious resource is its entrepreneurs - people like you. These are the intrepid souls who are trailblazing new possibilities. These are the few and the brave who know that paradise is on the far side of pain. But they also know that it takes Just-One-Last-Try to get there.

A final message about persistence: If your purpose is to genuinely help others, your will to persist will endure beyond your competition

If your only goal in becoming an entrepreneur is self-enrichment, we suggest you terminate your quest right now. If your goal is to genuinely help others, your success is almost certainly guaranteed.

Every great business has its roots in the desire to please, gratify and reward others. Every great business has the customer at its centre. Every great business ultimately uplifts the community it serves. Does yours? Because if you do not increase the well being of the people you serve, your business will die. And it will die soon. It's as simple as that.

One of the reasons why we approached Deloitte & Touche to sponsor this book is that they walk their talk of giving back to the community. Although Deloitte & Touche is a R1 Billion enterprise, they accept their responsibility to develop business at grassroots level.

Deloitte & Touche have formed a joint venture called Business Beat together with the Small Business Advisory Bureau, Eccles Associates Inc, a U.S. based consulting firm that specialises in small and medium size companies, ESKOM and Ntsika. Specifically, the vision of Business Beat is "to create vibrant economies within communities by unleashing creative potential and talent, identify opportunities, transfer skills and foster ownership through community participation."

In 1995, Deloitte & Touche saw that there were relatively few initiatives aimed at helping small and micro entrepreneurs on the ground. So they took action. As Charles Godfrey, Partner in Charge, Business Beat, says, "What began as a local monthly discussion forum has graduated into a fully integrated solution to SME development within our communities throughout South Africa". The informal business sector, through Business Beat, is getting to grips with key business issues, and is creating opportunities through the formation of joint ventures. We see our role as brokers of talent and resources. By facilitating the training, mentorship, financing and ongoing support of worthy candidates, we want to help the community plant, nurture and harvest the fruit of their economic success."

It seems to be working according to Vusi Nhlapo, President, Daveyton and Wattville Chamber. Nhlapo says, "By taking time to explain the fundamentals of economic and financial concepts to our members, Deloitte & Touche has helped us to get off the ground. There has been a real transfer of basic skills and understanding."

So here's our question to you: What will you do to reinvest in the community that supports you?

It's almost time to learn the Proven Parker 7-Step Formula for business success. But before you move on, here's an ancient Irish blessing to help you on your way:

May the road always rise to greet you
May the wind always be at your back
May the sun shine gently on your face
May the rain fall lightly on your fields
And, until we meet again,
May God hold you softly in the palm of his hand

Part Two

Getting Up & Running:

**How to grow rich through
The Proven Parker 7-Step Formula
for starting and managing your
business for maximum success**

You're pumped, you're motivated, you're ready to climb the mountain of success, wealth and independence. You've learnt how to keep yourself at the top of your game. You've got purpose, confidence, consistency, creativity and stamina. All you need now is the actual steps to making your dream happen. And that's exactly what we're going to give you.

The Proven Parker 7-Step Formula for business success has been refined by Eric over 30 years of experience, both as an entrepreneur and as a director of large companies. No-one in this country is in a better position than Eric Parker to guide you through the process of growing rich by starting and running your own business.

So work through the formula which follows. Don't rush it. The rest of your life may depend on it. Think about each point. Enjoy dreaming about achieving your goals as an entrepreneur.

By the end of this section, you will have the tools. Then all you need is the courage to break free, break through and build your own business.

The Proven Parker 7-Step Formula

Step One: To be successful, you must roll up your sleeves, be careful and eat, sleep, breathe the business.

"An employee sees things the way they are and asks "why?"
An entrepreneur sees things the way they never were and asks
"Why not?"

To kick off this section, we'll begin with the Ten Qualities of Extremely Successful Entrepreneurs. Before you start your mental journey with us, do a simple test on yourself. Rate yourself out of ten on each of the following ten qualities:

1. A willingness to work hard   _____
2. A desire to succeed   _____
3. A total commitment to the business   _____
4. A passion for the business   _____
5. Management and marketing ability   _____
6. Financial backing   _____
7. Strong 'people' skills   _____
8. Support from family   _____
9. The ability to handle setbacks   _____
10. A creative, flexible mind   _____

                                          Total _____

If you scored 85+, you're ready to rock and roll. This book will just reinforce your faith and sharpen your edge.
If you scored 75-84, you've got the right stuff but you need the

guidance we will provide you in the following pages.

If you scored less than 75, you've still got some major work to do. But that's why we've written this book - to help you find your way through the uncertainty and chaos of self-employment.

It's an all-or-nothing game

Be prepared to do whatever it takes during the first three years of the life of your new business. The business will dominate your life and the life of your family until it's strong enough to stand on its own two feet. In a way, your business is another addition to the family. In the beginning, it will be demanding, it will be delicate and it will keep you up at night. But like any new addition to the family, it will give you massive amounts of pleasure as you see it grow up.

The vital point of this first step is that you have to give your business all your attention. Just as you cannot "half give birth", you cannot "half-start" a business. Here are some fatal mistakes made by would-be entrepreneurs starting out:

1. I will keep my regular job and start my own business venture part-time.
2. I will let my spouse start the business and I will join the business as soon as it can afford me.
3. I will put up the capital and employ a manager to run it.

We promise you that if the business concept is good enough and the correct planning has been done, your business will be viable from day one. We are not saying you may not need financing. And we are not saying that you'll make a profit from day one. We're saying your business will start building momentum from the very beginning, as long as you are totally on board. It's an all-or-nothing game.

Forecasting your cashflow

During the course of the 7-Step Formula, we will take you through the management of your cashflow. Up front, however, we want to tell you that you need enough capital for the set-up costs - that is to cover the cost of the entrepreneur on board with the required business tools to do the job from day one.

These business tools include everything you need to run an effective business. While we will take you through the actual business tools you need, the core principle is that you dare not attempt to economize on the core elements of your business. Any concept that you are prepared to dedicate at least three to five years of your life in, is worth the investment required. With accurate planning and the application of the steps we'll share with you in this formula, your business will pay out within a reasonable time frame.

Look at it this way:

If you have a well-researched business concept and you work at it full time, with fire in your belly, then you must be able to make more money than you would working for a boss. If this is not the case, then your business is simply not viable.

Entrepreneur, Investor, Buyer Beware

Many would be entrepreneurs fail because they don't do enough homework on their business. They are suckered or seduced into a business by a smooth talking salesperson who takes their money and runs.

The second vital point of this first step is that you must research your business venture as though your life depends on it. It does. In the next step, we help you write your business plan. Use this plan to decide whether your business concept has the potential to give you the return you desire.

Don't be in a hurry. There is an old saying that is especially relevant to starting up a business: Decide in haste, Repent at leisure. So don't let anyone pressure you into making a decision before you're ready and before you've done your homework. Starting or buying a new business will be a magic time in your life if you get the launch right. It will be a tragic time if you get it wrong.

Remember, the careless and their money are quickly parted. The careful and their money multiply and multiply.

Warning!

Before you start or buy your new business, warn your family and those closest to you about what's going to happen to you and them.

Warn them about the sacrifices that will have to be made in the short term. Warn them about the stresses and strains that come with being your own boss. Warn them about the support they will all have to provide you as you take on the biggest challenge of your life.

You know what? If you're an entrepreneur, the desire to be your own boss runs in your veins. It's not just a way of making a livelihood, it's a way of life. Eric has put all his children into businesses. His daughter, Linda, has a physiotherapist practice and his sons, Barry and Greg, are joint owners of the Seattle Coffee Company. Every evening when Eric returns home from running his own company, he wants to know from his kids about what happened to their businesses that day. From Linda, he wants to know the number of patients she saw that day. And from the boys, he wants to know the daily turnovers of all the coffee shops. His wife, Val, often complains that the evening dinner often turns into a mini-board meeting with the members of family acting as directors of the board. And yet, being in business with each other has bonded the Parker family closer together.

Eric would have it no other way. He believes that starting a successful business delivers the ultimate high, especially in the early days while the business is taking shape.

Mike, on the other hand, has been an independent entrepreneur since 1 January 1993. He is still as hands on today as he was seven years ago. That doesn't mean that he hasn't delegated or outsourced many of the functions he used to perform. It simply means that his fingers are on every vital pulse of the business. He has seen so many people lose their businesses because they strayed from the first fundamental of business success: Up close and personal attention from day one to the day you sell the business or move on.

There is one other fact that will become very clear to you from the first day as an entrepreneur: There is no difference between Monday and Sunday. While you will need to give yourself a break sometimes to recharge your batteries, you can forget about the traditional weekend break. When it's your business, you never stop thinking about it. In fact, even when you're taking a break, you're still searching for ways to get better results. That's one of the main reasons why you need to take breaks - so you can think rather than do.

Starting lean and mean

At the start of this step, we told that you need enough capital to get going. Now we're going to tell you that you can minimize the capital required by starting lean and mean. In fact, even if you can afford to splash out on your launch, we recommend conserving your capital up front. What's more, if you start your business with a mindset of maximum efficiency, you're more likely to retain it throughout the entire life of your business. One of the golden threads running through all successful businesses is an almost fanatical focus on "sweating the overheads", ensuring that no capital is wasted on non-essentials.

The other advantages of starting lean and mean are that you will be able to make decisions quickly. You will have a tight rein on every aspect of the business. Interaction with employees will be direct, eliminating misunderstandings and communication gaps. This direct contact with employees is vital because in these early days, your business will be in its most dynamic phase. You and your business will be in fast-forward mode. You'll also be learning as you go along. The simpler your business structure, the better.

You will have so much on your plate that the discipline of daily "check lists" will be a mandatory management aid. A typical checklist may look like this:

Date _____

Priority No	Action	Completion Date
1.	Collect Debtors from "ABC"	_____
2.	Phone "D&J" for promised orders	_____
3.	Phone bank manager re overdraft	_____
4.	Send out o/s invoices	_____
5.	Order raw materials for new job	_____
6.	Approve advertising poster	_____
7.	Order stationery	_____
8.	Check petty cash	_____
9.	Arrange for wages on Thursday	_____
10.	Arrange for vat cheque on Friday	_____

Get into the discipline of writing everything down. Use checklists. There will be so much for you to do, you can't just leave it to memory.

What if you have no choice but to appoint a manager of your new business? Give your manager a stake in the business!

Although we discourage delegating the running of your new business to a manager, we understand that there may be certain situations where this is unavoidable. If you are forced to hire a manager, the most effective way of motivating your manager is to give him or her a stake in the business. If your manager has her personal well being tied up in the health of the business, she will act like an owner not just a hired hand.

We have also discovered that when it comes to really getting someone to commit to your business, you need to get them to invest some of their own money in the business. Nothing motivates someone to give it they've got like the fear of losing their own hard-earned cash. (See the session on staff relations)

Ultimately you are the champion of your business

There is one reality that we want you face in this first step to getting up and running: You are it!! There is no one else to blame for mistakes or things going wrong. It's your call. You are responsible. Whether you are a man or a woman, this new business is your baby. It's going to trip, stumble and fall. And you have to be there to pick it up, dust it off and send it back on its way. It is only your dream and your vision that will inspire the business to become all it can be. You will get frustrated, irritated, angry, anxious, despondent, enraged, depressed, frightened and fatigued. But you will also discover the ultimate excitement, energy, exhilaration, joy, achievement, satisfaction, fulfillment and growth.

Kentucky Fried Chicken had Colonel Saunders, McDonalds had Ray Kroc, Microsoft has Bill Gates, Sun International had Sol Kersner, Altron has Bill Venter, Nando's has Robbie Brozin, your business has YOU!

So go for it!! You may just make history! And here's a final magnificent quote from Theodore Roosevelt, a former president of the United States of America, to get you on your way:

"The credit belongs to the man who is actually in the arena; whose face is marred by dust and sweat and blood; who strives valiantly; who errs and comes short again and again; who knows the great enthusiasms, the great devotions, and spends himself in a worthy cause; who at the best knows in the end high achievement; and who at the worst, if he fails, at least fails while daring greatly.

Far better it is to dare mighty things, to win glorious triumphs, even though checkered by failure, than to rank with those poor spirits who neither enjoy much nor suffer much, because they live in the grey twilight that knows neither victory nor defeat."

The Proven Parker 7-Step Formula

Step Two: Making a Plan: how to construct a simple and workable business plan

"Plan your work and work your plan. If you fail to plan, you plan to fail"

Ancient Entrepreneur's Truth

The quality of your business plan will ultimately determine the quality of your future and that of your family

A note before you take this step: The business plan is written for YOU. You must be comfortable with it. It must a friendly, easy-to-use, simple guide to help you manage your business and, as importantly, measure your achievements. You must personally compile your business plan and take full ownership of it. Although you may need to use consultants or advisors, this is your future you are planning. The quality of your business plan will ultimately determine the quality of your future and that of your family.

Many entrepreneurs believe they need a business plan only to please the bank and investors. They get consultants or commercial mercenaries to write their business plan for them. *We're telling you now, that's a big mistake.*

You know why it's a mistake? First of all, because it's not really your plan, you will not really believe in it. You won't have the guidance and discipline that comes with your personal involvement in the plan. Secondly, when the bank receives a copy of the plan and interviews you, they'll rapidly establish that the plan isn't really yours. That will make it difficult, if not impossible, for you to acquire the support and financing you require.

The real test of a plan is twofold: Firstly, whether it can be used to easily answer the most important questions your banker may have. And secondly, whether it can answer the most important questions you may have. You see a great plan eliminates doubt and gives you confidence. And confidence is what makes entrepreneurs really successful.

How to select the right business – Follow your instinct but proceed with caution

The number one criteria for starting, buying or running a successful business is that you must truly love it. You must have an absolute passion for it.

So identify what business really turns you on. For Eric, it's working with people and providing them with the advice that will help them become successful. For Mike, it's getting people so excited that they motivate themselves to achieve their dreams. What does it for you? Do you have a hobby? Can you make money from your hobby?

In general, though, we would advise you to avoid areas in which you have little or no experience. They may seem exciting from the outside, but once you really become involved in them, you may find them barren.

To get your entrepreneurial juices flowing, here are 15 important questions for you to consider:

1. What business do I want to be in, and are my objectives clearly defined? What is my competitive advantage? Why will I be superior to my competitors in the eyes of my customers?
2. What sales must my business generate, firstly, to break even and, secondly, to give me a satisfactory return on my investment? Sales must be reported both in Rand terms and in standard unit terms.
3. Is the market that I am operating in large enough to sustain my projected growth plans? Will the market growth be sustainable over a long period of time? Is the market seasonable? Who are my competitors? Are my competitors likely to grow?
4. Are my customers accessible and can I distribute my product or service to them easily and economically?
5. How price sensitive is my market? Can my product or service

demand a price premium to ensure that achieve my targeted gross profit?

6. Can I afford all the operating costs needed to manufacture, market, distribute and administer the business and still make my desired return on investment? Do I have enough working capital to operate my business until I move out of the red into the black?

7. Can I afford to employ the best possible staff? What is my optimum staff complement? Where do I find the best staff? How do I keep the best staff?

8. Can I obtain the rights to a unique product or service from offshore companies? As long as this product or service is suited to local conditions, this can be a great competitive edge.

9. What is the legislation relating to my selected category? For instance, the security industry is regulated by a wide variety of associations, some of which are applicable to all security companies and some aimed at specialist categories. Many industries have self-regulating bodies, find out who they are and if they can add value to your business.

10. What can I learn from potential suppliers? Visit and interview your potential suppliers. Companies keen to obtain your business will often be able to give you invaluable information about the market and the industry.

11. Does the potential exist to develop a strong brand name? A brand is more than a marketing gimmick, a strong brand may turn into a substantial value on your balance sheet.

12. Will there be a substantial barrier to entry i.e. will my concept be easily copied if it proves successful? If this is the case, consider how you can raise those barriers to entry by delivering outstanding service and other unique benefits.

13. Will my required manufacturing plant and raw materials be freely available? Once consumers are excited about your product, you must be able to provide consistent supply.

14. Can I make a better return on my investment than if I had invested my capital in safer ways e.g. unit trusts, fixed deposits, property?

15. Will I be able to sell or exit my business easily? If I need the money, how easy will it be for me to get liquid?

Okay, the preceding 15 questions were just a warm-up. Are you ready for the real thing?

Note: even if you are not seriously considering starting up a business right now, work through each step as if you were. Think of the kind of business you would like to be in and then do the exercise. Think of it as a dress rehearsal for the real thing.

If you are seriously considering your own business right now, please work through each step thoroughly. Do your homework. Do your research. Treat the plan that follows as your lifeline. If you decide to take the ultimate plunge, it could very well be.

By the way, the following business plan outline is as relevant whether you are starting up or buying a business.

A final tip before you start your plan: Write your business plan in language that is alive and action oriented. Build conviction and passion into your plan. Anyone reading your plan, including you, should be excited by every word. You see, your business plan is not just a business document, it's a personal blueprint for success.

Outline of a Business Plan

1. **Executive Summary:** The executive summary provides a brief overview of the market in which your company will operate as well as the products or services you will deliver. Most importantly, the executive summary should describe the most appealing attributes of your business clearly and concisely. You should write this part of the plan as though it alone would attract investors to your business.

In the executive summary, you need to highlight your edge over similar existing businesses. This edge could be in the form of a unique patented product or service. Or it could be a niche market that has not been served before. Or it could be in the way you will market your product/service.

The driving principle here is that your business must not be a "me-too". It must stand out. And it must stand out in a meaningful way to the person who matters most, your prospective customer.

Remember, the greater your competitive advantages, the less risk your business faces. And the more likely your bank will be to lend you the money!

2. Business Objectives: A business objective is the result you want your company to obtain within a specified time frame. These objectives should be realistic and attainable. They must be backed up by facts, not fiction. It is, after all, the easiest thing in the world to become a millionaire on a spreadsheet.

Keep your business objectives limited to between three and five. Too many business objectives will destroy your focus.

You need to do your homework. Your objectives will direct everything else about your business. Remember: garbage in, garbage out, money lost.

3. The Business Concept (Description of your product or service)
Describe, in detail, the product/service that will form the basis of your business:

*   *Will you manufacture or purchase the product?*
    Manufacturing will require a larger capital outlay, due to investment in equipment. When purchasing the product, you will need to invest in stock. In both cases you will need suppliers to service you.

*   *Are you providing a service?*
    What is the nature of the service? What is the benefit it will deliver to customers? What is its competitive advantage?

*   *What is the extent of your range of products/services and will you add to this range?*
    Be careful when determining your range of products/services. Stay focused! You cannot be everything to everybody. Less is more. By trying to be everything, you may lose everything.

*   *How will you package your product/service?*
    Your packaging is an extension of the product itself. It is often the first impression that a prospect gets of your product. That's why it is so important that the way you package your product/service is attractive yet functional. If it does not turn the customer on, the chances are the customer won't buy it. The packaging of some

products is so distinctive, that the packaging almost becomes a reason to buy the product (think Pringles). Unique packaging can be patented.

Remember, in business, you do judge a book by its cover.

* *How will you deliver your service? Develop a separate "service plan"*
If you are providing a service, you need to focus on the tangible delivery of your service to the prospect. You need to demonstrate why your service delivery will win over customers. Develop a separate plan showing how you will gain the competitive edge through customer satisfaction. (see step 7 on Customer Care)

Your literature and presentation must be impeccable, colourful, high quality and professional.

* *How will you store your product?*
This will depend on the nature of your product. Is it perishable or not? Is the product big and bulky? You might need warehousing facilities. This can be rented or outsourced. If you are supplying customers, consider the difference between warehousing or delivering directly to the customer.

One of the realities of services marketing is that services can not be stored. To compensate for this, many service providers have special promotions in off peak time, like special rates on hotels in the off-season and on midnight flights. The objective of these promotions is to encourage usage because in the service business, you're selling time. And once that time has passed, you can't get it back. You need to work out when your service business will experience downtime and how you can compensate for this.

* *How will you distribute the product/service to your customers?*
What will it take to get your product from the point of manufacturing (or purchasing) to your end customer? Determine whether you will need vehicles and extra staff to manage distribution of the product. Distribution is all about getting the product to your customer - the way they want to receive it. It's all about speed, convenience and doing it better and faster than your competition. Efficient and reliable distribution of your

product/service alone may be a powerful competitive advantage in South Africa where service delivery is so bad.

* *How will you render after sales service?*
What does after sales service entail and where will it happen (e.g. at the customer's home or at your premises). If you provide guarantees, make sure that you can deliver on them.

Remember, customers buy relationships not just products or services. The more valuable your product or service is, the more important the relationship. Many entrepreneurs succeed in the beginning but then they fall down on after sales care. The customer wants to be taken care of.

Loyal customers will also become your biggest assets. So concentrate on doing whatever it takes to keep your customers happy.

* *What will your product or service cost to manufacture and distribute?*
You need to consider the cost of manufacturing every component and detail of your product from raw material to the distribution of the final finished product into the hands of the consumer.

In the case of services, you need to establish the cost of designing your service, packaging your service and delivering the service to the customer.

* *Can you patent and protect the unique benefits of your product?*
Make sure that you have registered your brand name. And patent anything that is patentable, from physical design to packaging.

* *Have you developed a compelling, distinctive brand name and and look?*
The most powerful way of ensuring the success of your business is to differentiate yourself effectively from the competition. Chances are that no matter what business you are in, you will be heading into a highly competitive marketplace. You need to stand out from the crowd by creating a unique Brand Identity that attracts customers to you.

The key criteria for building a Brand Identity are: Appeal to prospects, relevance, the right personality for the market, user friendliness and the offer of an important benefit that is not currently on offer by the competition.

A good brand is easily recognizable and its name must be easy to pronounce. Simplicity is the key to success. Consumers must remember it easily. This is what branding is all about: occupying the number one spot in a consumer's mind to ensure repeat sales. Another important consideration is whether the brand name can be protected or not. Intellectual property must be registered as soon as possible and must be difficult to copy. Generic names are difficult to register (for example, The Coffee Place is a generic name whereas Joe's Coffee Place is attached to a name and easier to protect). A good brand name cannot be copied easily (think Compaq, Intel, Coca-Cola and Nike).

4. The Market: You'd better know exactly whom you are selling to. You'd better know everything about who you're selling to. And you'd better know how you can keep on selling to them. If you don't have a clear picture of your market, it means you're flying blind. And if you're flying blind, you'll crash. It's as simple as that. There are too many people who go into business on a hunch or a whim. They think they see a gap in the market. But often, there's no market in the gap. So, up front, you need to clearly define your market:

- *Market size: Your Target market*
  What is the current size of the total market, and what is your coverage of it? Do you want to go after the whole market or just a segment of it? Remember, some of the most successful businesses in the world are niche businesses - businesses that dominate a very small sector of the total market.

  You may wish to increase your market coverage. Consider alternative uses for your product that will increase its use, and devise strategies to market these alternatives - think of Johnson's Baby Shampoo which is marketed as a shampoo for young children and as a gentle, everyday use shampoo for adults.
  Note: It is unlikely that you will be able to sell into the entire market, therefore you should target a viable sector of the market, which will be referred to as your target market from now on.

Your target market is the group of people who will be most receptive to your product or service. This is the group of people who you will have to know as well as your relatives. The better you know them, the better you will understand them. And the better you understand them, you better you will be able to sell to them.

You can also have more than one target market. For example, this book has two target markets: Firstly, the buyers for bookstores and businesses. Secondly, you - the reader. The first target market is known as the "trade" while the second target market is known as the end-consumer. We have a separate business plan for each group.

- *Market Growth*

  When considering your target market, you must choose one that has the potential to grow over time. This means that fads do not present a sound business opportunity, since its growth is not sustainable over the long term. Even if the market is static at present, there must be a potential for growth. Changes in consumer lifestyles are often a safe indication of market trends. For example, the latest trend towards convenience will most likely lead to growth in delivery concepts and ready to eat meals.

- *Market trends*

  Market growth and market trends are inter-related. If you can read the trends ahead of the competition, and you can take action, you can seize the initiative in your industry. That's why it's so important to stay in touch with developments in the marketplace and different trends in general. Lifestyle and economic changes do have a massive impact on the consumer market. Make sure that you stay in touch with these trends by reading popular literature. In this way, the mass media might provide you with more insight than some business publications! From this moment on, read everything and watch everything from the point of view of an explorer who is searching for the next big business breakthrough.

  You know why we got together to write this book? We watched

the market trends. We saw that the future of South Africa is in the hands of self-employed entrepreneurs. We saw that neither government nor big business could create jobs. We saw that big companies are down-sizing. We saw that many people just cannot be employed or re-employed in the formal business sector. We saw the huge entrepreneurial energy in South Africa. We also saw a gap in the market. We believe that no really motivating, fully comprehensive book on starting your own business had ever been launched in South Africa. We also saw this target market growing rapidly over time. We did our homework. We pooled our talents. We didn't waste time. And, presto, this book was born. We walk our talk.

- *Regional split*
  Where are you going to do business? Regionally, nationally or internationally? How much will it cost you to market your products nation-wide and do you have the resources? One of the biggest mistakes that new entrepreneurs make is that they try and expand too fast. Their own success can lead to their downfall.

  Is your product or service oriented towards the rural or urban areas, or both, and how will you adapt your approach?

  Also, how many competitors are already operational in the areas that you want to go into? How many outlets can successfully operate in one area?

  South Africa also has very diverse cultures and climates. It's almost like nine countries in one. For example, heating products simply do not sell in Kwazulu-Natal. Surfboards do not sell in Gauteng. Sushi (Japanese-style raw fish) doesn't sell in the Free State. So make sure that your product is acceptable to the region you're trying to develop.

  It is also important to determine what elements will contribute to an economically viable area, e.g. the number of economically active people, number of households, level of income, age and occupation of residents.

- *Market Seasonality*
  Most businesses experience some form of seasonality. Ice cream is

less popular in wintertime; entertainment gets a bigger slice during school holidays and so forth. It is important to factor the seasonality of your market into your business plan and consider its impact on your business. For example, what seasonal promotions will you have to run? What will be the impact on your cashflow and staff complement? What pricing strategy will you have to follow to optimise the upside of the in-season and minimise the downside of the off-season?

- *Competitive activity*
  Your competitors will always have a profound effect on your business. Try to anticipate what the competitor reaction to the introduction of your concept will be. Take into account the current competitor activity and how you can react to it.

  Any concept usually has at least two levels of competitors, namely direct and indirect competitors. If you have a burger place, your direct competitors will be the Wimpy's and BJ's of the world. Your indirect competitors are anyone else who operates in the food industry. You will need different strategies to counter the competition at these different levels. At any level, ensure that you are aware of what the competition is doing. Follow their ads, press announcements and promotions. Just reading the morning paper, listening to the radio and watching TV can give you a good fix on what the competition is doing.

  Remember, if you're going to work for yourself, you cannot switch off. Even when you're relaxing, you have to be alert to developments and opportunities.

* *What should your Pricing Strategy be? How much is your target market prepared to pay for your product/service?*
   How much should you charge for your product or service? That's one of the biggest decisions an entrepreneur will have to make. Well, the price you charge is a function of how unique your product is; how much the consumer really needs your product; how easy it is to get your product from another competitor; how many services you provide with the product; your after sales service and how well you've marketed yourself and your brand.

There are two basic ways of determining your pricing strategy: *Cost-Plus* or *Market-Driven*. *Cost-Plus* is when you calculate what it will cost to produce your product or service and then you add on what you believe is an acceptable margin. *Market-Driven* is when you price your product/service based on what the market believes it is worth. We are strong advocates of the Market-Driven Approach.

Warning: It often happens that an operator is scared of asking a higher price, when his customers will in fact be willing to pay more. Do physical research to establish what your target market will be prepared to pay, i.e. sell the product at the higher price to determine if the market will bear it. You will be amazed at the results. Don't sell yourself short!

- *What quantities will my target market purchase from me?*
  This is a difficult challenge for a new business. In the beginning, it's tough to forecast how the target market will react to your product. Yes, it can be costly to carry too much stock, but turning customers away due to out-of-stocks is even worse. Finding the balance will come from experience, and you will only be able to make accurate forecasts once you are operating. In the meantime, our advice is to carry sufficient stock to cover orders.
  Warning: If you let down a customer because you are out-of-stock, that customer will probably lose money because of you. That customer may never forgive you. What's more, that customer is going to talk about his bad experience to his associates.

- *What payment terms must I offer e.g. cash, 30 days, what settlement is required?*
  The terms you offer may be a function of your industry and customer expectations, i.e. know what your competitors are doing. But if you are going to offer terms, make sure that your cash flow can accommodate it. If you're going to offer terms, you had better make your bank manager your best friend because you're really going to need him.
  It may be worth your while to offer customers an incentive to pay quickly. This may take the form of a cash discount or other preferential treatment.

There is an old saying about cashflow that is highly relevant here: Turnover is for vanity. Profits are for sanity. And cashflow is reality.

5. Building a solid foundation: infrastructure required to manage your business

Just as you need a solid foundation for a building, so you need the right infrastructure for your business. This needs to be addressed ahead of time. Seriously, *many businesses fail because they become too successful.* Their infrastructure can't cope with their growth and so their business literally falls apart. Don't make that mistake. Clearly define what infrastructure will be required to run your business both in the short and long-term. Let's look at the different components of your business infrastructure:

- *Premises:* What is the physical capacity your business will require? What will be the optimal location for you in terms of closeness to your customers, major roads and the location of the competition.

   If you are thinking of starting a service or consulting business, premises may not be important because you visit the customer on their premises. Both Eric and Mike are constantly on the move as they travel to where their clients are.

- *Staff:* Remember the fundamental law of business: People buy People. This issue is so important that we dedicate an entire session to it later on. At this stage, though, here are the key issues you need to consider in your business plan: What is your ideal staffing complement in terms of the number of staff and their competency levels? Also, assess your current operation to determine where you may need special skills or where you may have "skill gaps". For example, you might discover that you will need a qualified buyer or a stronger financial person. Don't hesitate to invest in high quality staff.

- *Staff training and development:* Once you've appointed the right staff, you need to decide what will staff training entail in terms of content and time allocated to it. Also, determine who will take responsibility for training. This is a vital component in setting up your business and it deserves a high priority. If you neglect the skills and attitude development of your people, you will neglect the growth and development of your business. It's as simple as that. And yet, lack of staff training and development is one of the biggest mistakes made by entrepreneurs.

- *Equipment:* Determine the types of equipment that you will need and the specifications of this equipment. Where will you source it and at what price?

- *Systems and controls:* You will need the appropriate computer systems in your business to manage stock, point of sale and financial recording. These systems should provide you with the necessary information to run your business at an optimal level. Without the right systems, your business will soon end up in a mess. Get at least 2-3 companies to "pitch for your business". By that we mean, ask 2-3 companies to recommend the best systems for your business. The leading companies have had a lot of experience in helping new businesses get off the ground. Use their knowledge to help you. And before you hire them, check out their references.

  The four most feared words in the English language are "The computer is down". You don't want that to happen to you.

- *Operation manuals:* The operations manual is your business bible. It should contain all information pertaining to the running of the business. It should also form the basis of all training. It is your business blueprint. It is the A-Z of how you do business. It is a guide that serves as a constant reference for your employees.

  The operations manual is a vital document and you should invest the right amount of time in preparing it. If the manuals are not developed yet, make sure that you provide for its development in your business plan, allocating the necessary resources to it.

- *Transport:* Determine the requirements you will have in terms of vehicles and other methods of transport. Do you need to be close to the airport and major highways? Do you need to deliver goods to customers? Or can you outsource this function?

* *Warehousing:* Determine your warehousing requirements. How much space do you need and what will be the ideal location of your warehouse? What are your security needs?

6. What marketing do you need to develop your brand names and ensure you achieve your projected sales forecast? You need a marketing plan that will empower you to hit your sales targets and build your brand image in the mind of your target market. This aspect of your business is so important that we dedicate the whole of the next session to it.

7. Business Pre-Opening procedures checklist: We have included a detailed checklist in appendix 1 for your personal use. Outlined below are some of the elements that you need to consider:

- Registration of company (select type of company refer appendix)
- Name of company
- Registration of brand names
- Registration with statutory bodies (see appendix)
- Administration staff/outsourcing this function
- Open bank account
- Telephones
- Fax
- Photo copies
- Financial package
- Print stationery, letterheads etc.

8. Budgeting your ideas: At last, the brainstorming and thinking part of your business plan is over. Now you must translate your thoughts into a comprehensive, measurable budget to establish how much money (capital) you require to start the business, how much money you are going to make in the short term, and how you will generate an exciting return on your capital over the medium to long term.

As entrepreneurs we also want to know what 'return on sweat" we will achieve i.e. is all the extra effort going to be worthwhile because we will need to put in much more hours and stress than working for a boss.

THE BUSINESS PLAN AS A MANAGEMENT TOOL

Too often, it happens that an elaborate business plan is drawn up for the bank and investors, and then it ends up in a cupboard gathering dust. Instead, you should use the business plan as a management tool to keep track of your progress and benchmark your successes. Obviously, your business plan will also change as you go along. It is a dynamic tool that you should be constantly sharpening and tweaking. So, how can you use your business plan as a management tool?

- **The planning and management process: Discipline shall set you free.** Committing a strategy to paper requires discipline and forethought. It requires a big picture of your business before you commit your life to it. Many entrepreneurs lack this perspective as they run around putting out fires and reacting to crises that they could have pre-empted if they had the plan in the first place. Writing and rewriting your business plan will give you the mental discipline to take stock of the business and strategize for the future.

  In many ways, business is like any other game. Unless you have a firm "game-plan" before the match, you're going to come short. What's more, just like sports, you need to keep adjusting the plan to take into account new realities.

  The completed business plan should illustrate where you are, where you want to be and how to get there. You should constantly referring to your plan and tracking the progress you are making towards your goal.

  To illustrate our point even more explicitly, we believe your business plan is like a roadmap showing you how to get to a certain destination. So when you get a map from the AA, it details the path, the mileage, rest stops and the road conditions you will experience on the way to your destination.

  Inevitably, because business is an uncertain science, you will deviate from the plan during the year. Using the plan as a benchmark will help you in evaluating these deviations more objectively so you can get back on track fast.

- **Internal communications:** The best businesses are always transparent. We recommend publicizing your plan to your employees as far as possible. While there may be certain financial information that you want to keep secret, sharing your plan with your people will ensure everyone is on-board with the business vision. Your people can then accurately share this information with your customers. They will feel empowered. They will understand why you are asking them to do what they are doing. They will give you that little bit extra.

  You will also receive feedback from employees, and this two-way communication will help you make better decisions and run a more successful business.

- **The outside world:** An up to date, well-prepared business plan is a huge advantage when dealing with banks, creditors and investors. It projects a professional image and reflects well on your planning and management ability. Furthermore, because so few entrepreneurs have a well-developed plan, you will stand out from the crowd.

Phew! Take a breather. You've earned it

We congratulate you for having made it this far. You are obviously an entrepreneur who is serious about getting ahead. We promise you that a thoroughly prepared business plan will pole-vault you into success. Take control of it and take control of your destiny.

Do it now, practice your dress rehearsal: on the basis of what we've shared with you, write your own business plan. Nothing will help you learn what we've shared with you more powerfully than writing your own plan, even if you don't have all the pieces of the puzzle yet.

Okay, time to get sexy!!

The Proven Parker 7-Step Formula

Step Three: How to make your business sexy – designing and executing an exciting, eye-popping, stirring, alluring marketing programme.

"I get no kick from champagne,
Mere alcohol doesn't thrill me at all,
So tell me why should it be true
That I get a kick out of you?"

Cole Porter

By the time you are ready to start trading you have already invested a big chunk of your capital on tangible items such as shop fitting, equipment. signage and stock. Often entrepreneurs are tempted to start trading and just see how it goes without investing in their most important asset: their brand image. Well, it's is useless having a beautiful shop with the best equipment and shop fitting, but no customers. It's like winking at someone in the dark - you know you are winking but nobody else does. No-one will respond to you. You will become increasingly frustrated and eventually you will close up shop.

We promise you that no matter what business you want to launch, your most important asset will not be something concrete or tangible, it will be your image and reputation. It will be the perception your customers have of you. It will be the feelings they have towards you and your product/service. This is also known as brand goodwill or brand equity. And it will be the most valuable asset you can ever build.

We define marketing as doing whatever it takes to build a

relationship with your customers that is intimate, enduring, and mutually rewarding. In fact, think of someone you really wanted to get close to - maybe it was your wife, your husband, your boyfriend, your girlfriend or your fiancée. Think of what you did to get close to them and convince them that you were the right person for them. Well, you may not have known it at the time, but you were practicing the fine art of marketing.

And marketing is an art. When you are dealing with the human mind and heart, there is no such thing as an exact science. So while we will give you the insight that we have learnt over 50 years of combined marketing experience, you will have to go through some trial-and-error to discover the best formula for your business.

Here is our core belief: The most successful companies worldwide are the best marketers. Think Coca-Cola, Nike, Virgin, Castle, Liquifruit, Microsoft, Spurs, Nando's, Compaq, Levi's, The Sharks. **The bottom line is that the most important function of your business is to get and keep profitable customers.** Everything else is just a supporting act. So as you read these words, ask yourself how you can constantly romance your customers to buy from you and keep buying from you.

South African companies in general underspend on marketing. In franchising, for example, South African companies' average marketing expenditure is 1,8% of sales whereas in America it is 5% of sales. Many South African businesses consider marketing to be a luxury. They spend money on marketing as a means of last resort. And when business gets tough, they immediately cut back on their market expenditure. We believe in exactly the opposite: *Rule number 1 of any successful entrepreneur – Be an aggressive, innovative, intelligent marketer.*

The overall objective of marketing is to convince your customers and prospects that you will give them what they want more effectively than anyone else who is competing for their business. However, there are many components to this word – marketing:

- *Advertising:* Many people equate advertising with marketing, yet it is only one aspect of the marketing process. Advertising is the way you communicate to your customers through the media - newspapers, radio, TV, outdoor, leaflets placed in mailboxes, posters on poles etc.

Your advertising should perform a 4-part function summarized as **AIDA**

Awareness – your advertising must make customers aware of your product. It must get their attention.

Interest – your advertising must make them interested in finding out more about your product.

Desire – your advertising must make them want to buy your product.

Action – Your advertising must make them take action. They must go out and actually buy your product or service.

Your advertising must work in conjunction with other forms of promotion to really work effectively. These include sales promotion, direct marketing, public relations and personal selling. We will discuss each one in turn.

Just a note on "clever" advertising, while it is great if your ads get people talking, it is still important that it is product related. How many times have you seen a brilliant ad, but you can't remember the product it advertised?   Make sure that your advertising focuses on the product and its benefits.

- *Sales promotion:* Sales promotion can be defined as those promotional activities you perform to generate immediate sales of your product or service. So sales promotions can include competitions, incentive offers, sales, discounts, free gifts etc.

  A common mistake made with sales promotions is to promote only when sales are down. Rather try to "fish where the fish are". If you promote when sales are doing well, you will elevate your sales to an even higher level.

  Also bear in mind that promotion is not a synonym for discounting. Rather promote by adding value to the consumer. One example of this is "combo's", selling a combination of products at a price that the consumer perceives as good value. Rather than compromising on margins as you might with discounting, you are moving more products and increasing margins. Just visit any McDonalds to discover how to do this well.

- *Public relations(PR):* Nothing beats great PR to increase your visibility and credibility. Someone once said, "Advertising is what you pay for, PR is what you pray for!" The power of PR is that it is perceived by consumers as true. It appears in the press as editorial. People believe it because the newspaper or magazine is seen to be saying it, not you.

    There are many small, inexpensive PR agents around. Hire one or do your own PR, but make sure you get publicity. It's gold. In fact, we'll make a confession to you: one of the main reasons why we are writing this book is for its PR value. Anyone will tell you that you can't make a lot of money on books in South Africa. But the amount of publicity we will receive on this book is worth thousands of rands.

- *Direct Marketing:* Direct Marketing is when you send promotional material or communicate directly with the precise people who you want to become your customers. Direct marketing takes the form of letters and telephone calls to prospects. You can buy lists of potential customers from list brokers.

    Direct marketing can be very powerful because you are talking directly to the people who either are your customers or who will become your customers. And here's a vital point: Always be talking to your existing customers so that they don't leave you because of lack of interest. It's much cheaper to keep an existing customer than it is to attract new ones.

- *Personal Selling:* Personal selling is where you go face-to-face with customers and persuade them to buy your product. It is expensive and it is time consuming, but nothing can be as effective as one-on-one communication. Our recommendation, where appropriate, is that you identify who are your biggest customers/prospects and call on them to make the sale. As a rule of thumb, the bigger the value of what you have to sell, the more effective personal selling will be.

- *Distribution:* Distribution is often the "black sheep" of the marketing process. Yet fancy advertising campaigns are useless when your product is not on the shelves or when your store is understocked. You must have a plan for getting your product to the consumer and keeping it in front of the consumer.

- *Merchandising:* Merchandising refers to the way you show your product or service to the consumer. Always look for more exciting ways of merchandising your product. The new buzzword in retail is "shoppertainment". Consumers want to be entertained while shopping. Put the fun back into shopping through your merchandising.

- *Packaging:* The packaging of your product is a valuable extension of your marketing message. Make sure that it has the same "feel" as the rest of your marketing campaign. If your marketing campaign has a high-tech feel, this must be reflected in packaging that has a high-tech look i.e. metallic and aerodynamic. Of course, the packaging must also be functional and user-friendly.

- *Corporate/Brand image:* The corporate or brand image is the overall image that customers will have of your company and brand. A common mistake made by many entrepreneurs is that they do not sustain a common look across all their activities. So keep your corporate image consistent, from stationary to staff uniforms. Every aspect of your business is an opportunity to strengthen your corporate image. Use it and reap.

- *After sales service and Customer Care:* We consider service and customer care important enough to devote a whole session to it. At this stage, we'll just say that customer care is as important to your business as love is to your family. Your customers must believe that you really care deeply about their welfare. And this care must be demonstrated in all their interactions with you.

  One of the most important factors in after sales service is to only make promises that you can keep. This is one of the biggest reasons for the failure of businesses - they are so eager to get the business, they make commitments they cannot honour. And they pay the price by losing the customer.

- *Price strategy:* We spoke about pricing in the business plan. However, your pricing is also a powerful marketing tool because of what it says about your product or service. Do you want to be positioned at the bottom of the market? Or do you want to be perceived as a premium quality sales or service provider? As a rule of thumb, the more unique you are and the more value you offer to the customer, the higher the prices you will be able to charge.

  Remember, if you position yourself as a discounter or "cheapie", your margins are going to be very thin. And thin margins mean a very hard life no matter how good you are.

  An effective pricing strategy also depends on good buying. Do your homework and make sure that you buy at the best prices.

- *Staff image and behaviour:* **Your staff are your representatives and ambassadors to the buying public.** They must understand what you expect from them and they must understand what the customer expects of them. For example, you don't expect the same level of service and attention at a fast food restaurant as you do at a 5-star restaurant. But you do expect courtesy, friendliness, and cleanliness from your fast food restaurant employee.

It takes time so have faith: Six simple steps:

Many inexperienced entrepreneurs expect too much from marketing in too short a time, e.g. they place one small advertisement in the paper or they distribute one leaflet and they expect immediate and significant increases in sales. When the results do not materialize, they lose faith. Remember, perseverance conquers all. The right marketing campaign is consistent communication directed in the right media at the right price to the right people at the right level over a sustained period of time.

From our experience, we have often found that entrepreneurs have not developed a marketing culture in the company because they don't know how and don't want to admit it. So here are six simple steps to follow when building an effective marketing plan:

Step 1: Establish your marketing budget

You must establish the amount of money you are prepared to spend on marketing. This is an important amount because it will help you formulate your budget. There is no magic formula that establishes the right amount but as a guideline it should be between 3% and 5% of your forecasted sales depending on your projected gross profit e.g.

Gross Profit	Marketing as percentage of sales
60% or more	5%
50%	4%
30%	3%

Remember marketing is not an expense but an investment because: -
i.   With good marketing you will achieve higher sales at higher price levels
ii. Your brand name will become a valuable asset in your balance sheet - e.g., How much value would you put on the on the Coca-Cola brand name?

> If you think that you are saving money by cutting down on marketing, it's the same as thinking that you will win time by stopping your watch. Sooner or later this mistake will catch up with you.

Both of us invest big chunks of our own capital in marketing our services. In fact, we spend even more when times are tough because we know the competition is backing down. As a result, we are both perceived as the leaders in our fields. Our point here is that success in business is a function of how others think of you. If you are constantly in front of their eyes, day in and day out, you and your business will stand out. Every Rand you invest in marketing is an investment in your most valuable business attribute – your brand or corporate image. As a rule, if you're in doubt, overinvest in marketing.

So go ahead, work out your marketing budget. This step means that you have to know what your sales and margins are going to be. Of course, we know you prepared your overall business plan from the previous session. If you haven't go back and do it.

Step 2: Understand the market in which you operate and select the segment you want to sell to:

As an example let us imagine we are selling motor cars to the South African market. It is impossible to produce one motor car that will appeal to everyone in the market e.g. an Opel Corsa might be just ideal for a university student but it would be useless for a taxi owner. We can segment the South African car market according to the following demographics-

- Age
- Sex
- Income bracket
- Education levels
- Language
- Urban/rural
- Occupation
- Aspirations
- Lifestyle
- Tastes

Now lets assume we would like to sell to the upper income bracket. We can still break that category down by age e.g.

Mercedes Benz would appeal to the older more conservative consumer while BMW would appeal to the younger flashier consumer. Therefore the Mercedes Benz target market might be the older more conservative customer in the upper income bracket.

As another example, Eric defines his target market for Seattle Coffee Company as upper income, urban consumers who love good coffee and appreciate the finer things in life. Mike defines his target market as ambitious, progressive urban consumers of all ages who really want to maximize their own potential and be the best they can be.

Now go ahead: segment your market and select your target market i.e. the most viable segment for your product.

Step 3: Positioning your service or product: the most important marketing decision you'll ever make.

Powerful, successful marketers position their company/brand so that their selected target market will purchase from them and only them, forever and ever.

For example, Coca Cola stands for delicious liquid refreshment;

BMW stands for sheer driving pleasure; Nike stands for the athlete's sportswear; Mike Lipkin stands for high-energy inspiration and fun. Seattle Coffee Company stands for classic coffee done anyway you like it. What do you or your business stand for?

In order to position your product or your service, you have to pinpoint your target market's needs, values and desires. Then you need to develop and position your product or service to satisfy those needs. Your advertising, promotion and everything else about your business must then communicate your positioning to the consumer.

Remember that positioning is all about consumer perceptions. When deciding on how to position your product, imagine how you want consumers to perceive it. Focus on benefits that consumers find meaningful and attractive. And, as importantly, focus on the benefits that you can offer better than your competition. Always market from your strengths and never try and be what you are not.

It is also never too late to reposition a brand, i.e. change your positioning, providing it is done right. Sasol went from ultra conservative and elitist to windy-windy in the space of one ad!

The three most important words when it comes to positioning are focus, focus, focus. Once you have decided on your positioning, ensure that every interaction with your customers reinforces this positioning - from the way you answer the phone to the message at the bottom of your invoices. Seize every opportunity to forcefully communicate what you stand for in the mind of the customer.

Step 4: Select the best, most cost-effective way of connecting with your target market

You know who your target market is and what you want to tell them - now you must select the best way of connecting with them. Tools at your disposal include:

- **Advertising:** If you select advertising, you must select the most appropriate, most cost effective media to reach your target market. In the case of Mercedes Benz, the best media may be leading business publications and programmes as well as travel and high class home and leisure publications. In the case of your local restaurant, it may be the local knock&drop newspaper. In the case of NuMetro Cinemas, it may be the regional newspapers such as the Argus or the Star.

- **Personal selling:** This entails you and your representatives calling directly on your target market. This approach is mainly used in service industries like insurance, financial planning, computers, fleet sales and sales to corporate buyers.

- **Public relations:** As we said earlier on, this is an extremely powerful tool. However, the media will only give you space or time if you have something unique, meaningful or newsworthy to say. Remember, the media have to provide their readers, listeners or viewers with news that they will find interesting. So find the right angle and go for it.

  Here's another tip: if you run advertising in a medium, they will be more willing to give you editorial coverage. So ask for it.

- **Sales Promotion (SP):** Sales Promotion is useful when you want to generate immediate response. It should be used in conjunction with your other promotional tools. SP could take the form of a free offer, a discount, an incentive such as a holiday, or a limited time offer. Mike often offers delegates to his seminars a free audiocassette as an "early bird" offer to get them to book before a certain date.

- **Direct marketing:** This tool is useful when you can acquire quality lists of your prospects. It is usually more appropriate for high value items. For example, if you are selling photocopiers, you would want a list of equipment buyers for companies. If you can get hold of a list of these buyers, you eliminate the wastage of talking to people who are not your target market.

- **The Internet:** This is an increasingly important tool as consumers become more used to the net. Some of the most successful businesses in the world are now concluded entirely on the net. So find someone who knows about the net. And get your own website designed. Then include your own website address in all your promotional activities. And by the way, if you want to visit Mike's website, you can click on www.mikelipkin.com

- **Sponsorships:** This option is usually for those businesses that are already up and running. It is an add-on to other forms of promotion. If sponsorship is used correctly, it can provide substantial media exposure for the sponsor. Think of Nike sponsoring the Springbok Rugby Team or Rothmans sponsoring the Rothman's Cup.

By the way, you don't need a lot of money to run a great marketing campaign. What you need is creative thought and the willingness to do whatever it takes to get your message through. So whatever your marketing budget, adapt your actions accordingly. Some of the best marketing campaigns in the world were executed on a shoestring budget.

Step 5: Implement your marketing programme

Now that you are ready to implement your marketing programme, remember that consistent promotional activity in a tight range of selected media is better than inconsistent efforts in numerous media. A rifle shot approach where you dominate one medium works better than a shotgun approach trying to cover all media. This is another mistake that many would-be entrepreneurs make - They try be all things to all people in all places.

Once again, you can see that marketing is about focus, discipline, consistency and plain damn blood, sweat and tears.

Finally, scrutinize all your other marketing activities to ensure they support your positioning and marketing campaign. This additional activity could include: -

- Staff uniforms
- Vehicle design
- Signage
- Packaging
- Corporate stationery
- Letterheads
- Website

Step 6: Measure your marketing activity

There is an old business saying that says, "What cannot be measured cannot be managed". It is absolutely imperative that you measure the success of all your marketing activities. Although successful marketing often results out of trial and error, you can minimize your "error" by developing what works and discontinuing what doesn't. We cannot overemphasize the importance of testing and measuring results.

Here are some ways of measuring your marketing efforts:

- Increase in sales after marketing campaign
- Increase in phone calls or visits
- Market research e.g. you can buy questions on a regular survey among your target market at a relatively low price and it will help you measure increases or decreases in awareness of your company or brand.
- When people visit your store or call you for information, ask them how they heard about your company, product or service.
- Do your own face-to-face and telephone surveys among customers and prospects. Confine your questionnaire to 2-3 vital questions about your business.

Now, as a result of this session, prepare your own basic 6-step marketing plan. Ensure that it plugs into your overall business plan. Be creative, but be focused and disciplined. Have some fun. Think of how you can really make your business sexy.

To help you prepare a powerful business or marketing plan, here are some resources you may find useful:

Institute of Marketing Management	(011) 482-1419
South African Advertising Research Foundation	(011) 463-5340
Market Research Africa	(011) 495-3200
Markinor (Market Research Company)	(011) 886-6469
Franchise Association of Southern Africa	(011) 484-1285/6/7
Department of Trade and Industry	(012) 310-9791

Go for it and good luck!!

The Proven Parker 7-Step Formula

Step Four: How to generate the capital you need simply and painlessly

"Sorry Honey, It takes money to make money and I don't have the money to make the money".
The biggest excuse in the world for not starting your own business.

Whenever we talk to people about why they don't start their own business, the most common excuse we hear is, "I don't have the money". Well, if you are truly committed to starting your own business, you'll find a way or make a way of getting the money. But here's the problem: *All our lives we are encouraged and taught to invest in CASH ABSORBERS and not CASH GENERATORS.*

CASH ABSORBERS are those expenses that absorb your cash like the Karoo in the rain. An example of a CASH ABSORBER is a brand new motor car. First of all, it costs a fortune. Then the day you drive it out of the showroom it loses approximately 20% of its value. The interest rate makes the monthly payments even more exorbitant, not to mention the cost of insurance, maintenance and, of course, the essential state of the art sound system. This car will absorb your cash like a vampire around your throat. Or to put it a tamer way, you are committing yourself to a substantial negative return on investment. To tell you the truth, you are committing yourself to a lifetime of financial struggle.

You know what, even now, both of us try and avoid Cash Absorbers as far as possible. As a habit, both of us are still investing as much capital as possible in CASH GENERATORS. For example, the lease on Mike's wife's car recently ended. Instead of buying a new car,

Mike simply refinanced the existing car. After all, the car is only four years old. It has done limited mileage. It's a Volkswagen Jetta so it has a lifespan of at least a couple more years. So now, Mike has the cash to invest in his business and he still has the financing costs to write off against tax. (Mike's wife works in the business).

A CASH GENERATOR is a vibrant investment that will generate cash for you. And, of course, the ultimate example of a CASH GENERATOR is your own business. A successful business will not only pay your salary, but it will also give you a highly favourable return on your investment. And, if you want to sell it one day, you should realize a hefty capital gain on your initial start-up cost.

So what's our point? Simply this: *Get into the habit now of investing as much as you can in Cash Generators and minimize what you put into Cash Absorbers.* You'll be amazed at how much cash you can save.

Okay, let us now consider three examples of how potential entrepreneurs raised capital to start their own businesses.

First Example: Linda, the disciplined 21 year old

Linda was 21 and recently qualified with a BCom (Marketing). She had just been employed as a product manager at a large fruit juice company. Linda lived with her parents and also had a second job moonlighting as a waitress at the local fish restaurant. Linda was determined to start her own business and so she set herself the goal of saving sufficient capital within 3 years. This is how she did it:-

Saving from salary approx. R4 000 per month	R150 000
Interest	R 30 000
Saving from waitressing	R 70 000
Total	R250 000

Linda went to visit her bank manager who was very impressed with her dedication and consistency. He told Linda that he would back her in the business to the tune of 60% of the total capital

Linda's capital	R250 000
Bank loan	R375 000
	R625 000

Linda could now go and plan to purchase or establish a business up to the value of R625 000. That's a nice sized business. And R625, 000 in capital is a lot of money by anyone's standards. So it can be done. Many young people are sceptical of approaching the bank. But the bank will consider you favourably if you have a good plan, like Linda had.

Warning: Make sure that you maintain a spotless credit record. Missing one payment on that clothing account can taint your credit record! And it could make raising capital tougher than it needs to be.

Second Example: Fred, the 50-year-old unemployed man

Fred was 50 years old and in good health. However, due to tough economic times his company had performed poorly. Fred had been retrenched with a package equal to 1 year's earnings. At first Fred felt confident that he would be re-employed rapidly and that the retrenchment package would be a bonus. However, six months later Fred had still not found employment. Time was running out for Fred. And he knew it. He came to the correct realization that he would probably never be employed in a large company again. Fred knew that he had to start his own business.

What's more, in addition to his retrenchment package, Fred had almost paid off his house, his car was fully paid for and he had his pension and two relevant annuities. In other words, Fred had built up some sizable assets over the years.

NOW Fred's dilemma WAS: does he put up his hard-earned assets to secure a loan?

What do you think? Well, we believe Fred has no option. He is too young to retire and his assets are not sufficient to sustain him in old age. He is also unlikely to get a job working for a company again. In other words, his only option is self-employment. At 50 with good health, his most productive years are probably still ahead of him. Obviously he needs to be extremely cautious but he needs to acquire or establish a business he can build over time.

And by the way, did you know that some of the world's most

successful entrepreneurs only started their businesses over 50. Just to name two: Ray Krok took over McDonalds in his fifties. Colonel Saunders started Kentucky Fried Chicken in his sixties.

Third Example: Monty, the highly motivated 35 year old marketer with a dream

Monty was a successful marketer with a senior position at a leading manufacturing company. However, although he was earning a good salary, he carried a lot of debt. He was still paying a large bond, his two children were in a private school and his wife wasn't working.

One day Monty was reading an overseas business magazine where he read about a new computer software package that had been successfully introduced into the American market. He followed up with the company which launched the package in the United States and discovered that they had not yet appointed a representative in South Africa. After doing his homework, Monty believed the package would do well in South Africa.

He approached the American company and requested the rights for the package in South Africa. Based on his track record, they agreed to give him the rights for a six month period after which his performance would be reviewed. Part of the deal, however, was that Monty had to develop the South African market at his own expense.

Monty had the skill and the determination to launch the business but he had zero capital. Furthermore, even his cashflow was stretched because of the debt that he carried. What would you do? Monty had an excellent, secure job making good money. Financially, he was extremely vulnerable. And this computer software package was untried in the South African market.

Would you put it all on the line? Monty was in what we call a "Moment of Destiny". He could go out and pursue his dream. Or, he could go back to the Comfort Zone. Well, Monty chose to pursue his dream. He compiled a superb, captivating business plan. He presented it to a combination of venture capitalists and bankers. They bought into him and his dream. He gave the business everything he had. And he made it big.

What's our point? If you have the desire, the dream, the discipline and the courage, you'll always find a way of raising the capital.

There are investors who are constantly looking for great ideas to invest in. Now, more than ever, South Africa is a land of opportunity for turned-on entrepreneurs with exciting business plans.

So never use money as an excuse not to start your own business ever again!!

The preceding three examples are conventional ways of raising capital. However, we can also think of creative ways such as the following:

You might decide to make 30% of your business available to family and friends. You can then approach these people with a plan where they supply the capital in return for a share in your business. Built into the plan could be an agreement that, at a certain point in time, they can sell the shares to you at a price that would give them a higher return on their money than other conventional investments.

Another route is the joint venture option, where you retain 49 % of the business and sell the other 51 % to a business partner or investor. Having a 49 % stake in a viable business should still beat being a salaried employee!

After reading this section, we hope you now have confidence that if you really want to start your own business you can find a way to raise the capital. You may need to drive a "skedonk" for a little while and work part time, but we assure you that these moderate sacrifices will be well worth it in the end.

The Proven Parker 7-Step Formula

Step Five: Control your cash flow because cash is king – you can't carry on running your business without money in the bank.

"Annual income twenty pounds, annual expenditure nineteen nineteen six, result happiness. Annual income twenty pounds, annual expenditure twenty pounds ought and six, result misery"

Charles Dickens

Imagine turning on your TV and watching a cricket match between South Africa and Australia. Jonty is batting and there's a great deal of activity however nobody has bothered to keep the score. Nobody is clear what Australia has scored and how many runs South Africa must score to win. We know you'll agree with us that the game would become meaningless. There would be chaos and you'd switch off the TV.

Running your business without accurate accounts is the same as playing cricket without the score. Your accountant does the same job as the scorer does in cricket. He records the performance of the business and presents it to you in a format that you will understand. And just like every run counts in Cricket, so every rand counts in your business.

To continue the cricket analogy further, when South Africa went into bat, they had a target to achieve (they had to beat Australia's score). And when you start your business you have a very clear target to beat - your budget.

So let's list the activities you can expect from your accountant.

Before you open your business:

- Register your business as a (Pty) Co, closed corporation, a partnership or a sole trader (see appendix 1). Register your business with all the statutory bodies e.g. The Receiver of Revenue etc. (see appendix 1).
- Open a bank account and help you secure the necessary loans and overdraft facilities. (We would like to make a point here, get rid of your loans and overdrafts as soon as possible. With the high interest rates that prevail in South Africa, interest on borrowed money can become a major expense. If you want to sleep easy at night, get rid of your debt as soon as possible.)
- Help you prepare a budget. A budget is prepared in advance and is the best estimate you can make of how your business will perform for at least the first year of operation. The budget will be set out like an income and expenditure account and will include your estimated sales, mark ups, gross profit and all the projected fixed and variable expenses ending with your estimated profits. This will be the yardstick by which you can measure how your business is running. If you are well below or well above budget, you will then make the necessary adjustments.
- Take out suitable insurance policies for your business.

After your business has opened:

- Set up a mechanism to record your daily business transactions e.g. sales, cash receipts, purchases and all expenses.
- Open a set of books (now recorded on your computer) e.g. cash book, journals, petty cash etc. This will most likely entail the purchase and installment of a software package suitable for recording and presenting of your financial results.
- Arrange to present your accounts to you on at least a monthly basis. You should receive a package consisting of an income and expenditure statement, a cash flow statement and a balance sheet not more than 10 days after the end of the month.
- You should insist on receiving the following information on a daily basis –

- – daily sales
- – gross profit
- – daily cash flow statement
- As your understanding of your accounts grows, you will come to appreciate ratios such as the liquidity ratio, staff cost Vs sales, rent Vs turnover, and other ratios relevant to your business.

We can't stress the importance of cash flow strongly enough. Most entrepreneurs put a great deal of emphasis on sales and not enough effort into the mastery of cash flow. This can be described as the "sales mentality". You must understand that sales DO NOT equal cash. If you are running a business today the first thing you need to check every morning is your CASH FLOW - Do you have sufficient funds to cover your expenses at least 2-3 months in advance?

If you don't master your cashflow, you will stagger from crisis to crisis as you battle to meet your salary, wages and expenses bill every month. You will learn to hate your bank manager as he tells you that you are over your credit limit and he won't honour any more of your cheques. You will break into cold sweats as you run around trying to collect outstanding payments from your customers. And, most importantly, you will take your eye off your business while you struggle to survive financially.

Two final warnings:

First warning: Remember at school, the scorer for the 1st team was normally the straight "A" student who had little ball ability and could not bat or bowl. What would happen if you made the scorer the captain of the team? Well, he would probably use his experience as a scorer to set ideal field placing and he would probably stop some runs being scored by the opposition, but he could not make them. He certainly wouldn't be the player who consistently leads the team to victory through inspired play.

In business, expect your accountant to be like a scorer. He may be conservative and effective at saving money, but he could lack the flair and drive of an entrepreneur. Pay attention to what he says but be careful he doesn't cramp your style.

Second warning: Choose your accountant very carefully. Many entrepreneurs, including us, are not experts at managing money. We don't know all the "tricks of the trade". Managing cashflow, especially when your business begins to grow, is a highly complex art. So invest time finding the right accountant. Make sure you check his references. Make sure you can get along with him. And make sure he has a good feel for your business. You must be able to communicate with your accountant. We promise you there will be times when, after your family, he will be the most important person in your life.

The Proven Parker 7-Step Formula

Step Six: Choose your team carefully, turn your team members on and keep them happy by taking great care of them.

"People are made up of 99% emotion and 1% reason. Take care of their hearts and their heads will follow"

Joy Madison

You arrive at work and turn on the machines - they work away day-in and day-out, producing a fixed quantity at a fixed quality. If they break down, it is simple to trace the problem and fix it. When your machines are old and fully depreciated, you simply replace them with new and improved models.

Your people are totally different - they can be complex, moody, temperamental, unpredictable and often secretive and insecure. They are known to report late, steal, break things, strike, sulk or just go slow That's just the way it is. And often it has a lot to do with the way you treat them.

On the other hand, you will have people who treat the business as if it is their own, work overtime, care, smile, go the extra mile and dedicate themselves to excellence. These are your stars. When you are lucky enough to get these people, do whatever it takes to keep them, motivate them and reward them. Give these stars all the recognition in the world, stroke them, massage their egos, boost their paycheques - they are the reason why your business will thrive. Without them, you're deadmeat - we just can't say it any simpler than that.

We promise you that at least 80% of the problems your business will face will be people related.

One of the defining qualities of great entrepreneurs is their ability to spot and hire the right people – often they work on gut feel. But they back up their gut feel by checking out these people with great care. No-one can give you gut-feel, but we can give you some tips on how to check out your most important assets:

- **Check references** – don't only check the references given to you, because these people were probably pre-conditioned. Phone and check references not supplied. When you check a reference, be prepared by having a well thought out series of questions you would like answered.

- **Consider conducting psychometric or personality tests** – These tests are readily available and they are inexpensive. One well-known entrepreneur with whom we have worked even puts all her potential staff and franchisees through a hand writing analysis. When we asked her why, she said it was because she had her own handwriting analyzed and was amazed how accurate it was.

- **Match the personality and culture of the candidate to that of your company** – A company is like an extended family to its staff. It is a group of people who behave in a certain way; they have certain beliefs, values and desires; and they live with each other at least eight hours a day. In other words, every company, no matter how small, has its own culture. Some people may fit in and others won't. Some people might have all the technical skills but they won't fit into your company. It is therefore vital to try matching the potential employee's personality to the personality of your company.

- **Master the art of interviewing** – The job interview is the most important meeting you will ever have with your employee. It's where you ultimately decide whether you are going to build a relationship with this person or not. It's almost like deciding whether you want to marry someone after one meeting. We recommend that you have other staffmembers interview job candidates. Get a second, third and fourth opinion. And decide on what kind of questions you are going to ask the candidate before the interview. Remember: In this country, once you hire someone, it could be for keeps.

- **Give the candidate an assignment** – One of the most effective ways to choose the right people is to ask them to prepare an assignment or presentation for presentation to you at a second interview. In this way, you will get an actual taste of what this person can do. In effect, you are asking the person to pitch for the job the way you pitch for your customer's accounts.

Warning:
Small companies often fail to do the basics because they don't have the resources of a big company. We find that these smaller operations often don't bother with letters of appointment, leave registers, grievance procedures and other legal and procedural aspects. However, they are not above labour legislation. In fact, smaller companies have to take special care in legalities, since they do not have large in-house legal departments to handle any queries and cases that may come up. As we all know, legal fees alone can bankrupt you. So avoid landing yourself in legal disputes by handling human resources in a professional way.

You've chosen your team well, now here are nine ways of turning your "team members" on and keeping them happy:

i. *Each team member should have a clear, updated job description with well-defined accountabilities and levels of authorisation.* However, don't create rigid reporting systems that will stifle creativity. Promote a culture of participation, innovation and sharing.

ii. *Team members should be encouraged to take ownership of their business unit,* section or area. They must be encouraged to take total responsibility. In return, you must treat them as partners. Ask them for their input and advice. Consult with them on changes. Involve them as deeply as possible in all aspects of the business.

iii. *It has been said that human beings can never get enough recognition.* We all hunger for praise, compliments and being somebody special. So honour, respect and stroke those team members who earn it. And do it with sincerity and integrity. Go out of your way to catch people doing something right. Celebrate outstanding achievements.

iv. *If one of your team members has performed below expectations, don't be afraid to face it with her.* But apply dignified, constructive criticism of the action not of the person. One of the biggest causes of staff dissatisfaction is the way they are criticised at work. So here's a valuable technique called the "Motivational Sandwich". If one of your team members needs criticism, first praise his performance over time, then criticise the action and state your desired performance levels, then praise the person and highlight your expectations for the future.

v. *Always encourage your team members to talk to you.* Make it clear that no idea is a bad idea. Very often, your staff will be more in touch with customer needs because they are in contact with the customer all day. Your staff can be your most valuable market research and consulting resource. You may even wish to set up rewards for feedback and ideas.

vi. *Be prepared to invest time and money developing your team members as your company grows.* Encourage your staff to attend seminars and study further if necessary. Tell them you'll either match their investment in their education or you'll pay for it if they achieve "pass" marks.

vii. *Communicate regularly with your staff.* Hold regular meetings and tell your staff about the company and your plans for future growth. Many entrepreneurs make the mistake of being "loners" and just treating their team members as hired hands. Remember, you're the coach and team captain. Your team members are relying on you for information and inspiration.

viii. *Build a team spirit.* At certain times, we believe you should socialise with your staff, away from the work environment. You could invite your staff to your house for a braai, or arrange a sports day or a picnic where they can bring their families. Or you could organize a "Bosberraad" where you take your key people away for a couple of days and talk about the business and ways you can make it more effective.

ix. ***Finally, and most importantly, Don't be Greedy.*** When your company starts to do well, share the success with your staff. Remember, they have helped you to get there, and if you share your success you will reinforce their feelings of ownership. We promise you that the more you give away, the more you will make. Ultimately, whatever the textbooks say, nothing motivates people like a share of the profits. What's more, when you share the profits, make a big deal out of it. Let people know how much you appreciate their contribution as you hand them their magical envelopes.

Although we know that you will do everything to sustain a healthy relationship with your people, Murphy's Law will hit you: things can go wrong so keep abreast of the latest labour legislation. Ensure that you know the policies on maternity leave, raises and sick leave, etc. Keep your staff record up to date e.g. keep your leave records up to date because unclaimed leave can become a big liability to your company.

Without question, our most successful corporate clients have one golden denominator: turned-on people. There is simply no substitute for this kind of competitive advantage. In fact, Mike believes that one of the reasons why he has been successful is the quality and motivation of people working with him. As an example, here's a testimonial about his personal assistant, Marion Crouwkamp, e-mailed to him by Shan King of Anglo Gold: "Thank you very much for responding to me so quickly. Wow! Talk about being motivated. Mike, you have a star supporting you. That's what I call Teamwork. Well done, Marion!"

In the USA, some large companies even provide medical aid to temporary workers like students working in the stores. So from the start we suggest you hire the best possible staff, pay well above the average and share your success with them.

Onwards and upwards.

The Proven Parker 7-Step Formula

Step Seven: Love your customers as they have never been loved before! Take their breath away! Amaze them! Delight them! Over and over again.

"A great lover is not someone who has a different partner every night. A great lover is someone who makes the same partner feel like a different partner every night"

Daphne du Maurier

Think back over the last three months and remember a time when a company really exceeded your service expectations. Having difficulty recalling such a moment? It's not surprising, because in the Linda King-Taylor customer care survey conducted in 25 countries, South Africa came second last. So what do you think? Is this a problem?

Not if you're a true, blue entrepreneur. It's a massive opportunity! In fact, it's probably the biggest reason why you're going to succeed, right? You're going to introduce a level of service unprecedented in your industry, right? You're going to amaze, astound and delight your customers, right? We hope your answer is yes! yes! yes! Because great service alone may be enough to give you the competitive edge. If your industry is anything like most the industries in South Africa, your competitors are probably delivering below standard service. All you have to do to set yourself apart from the herd and lift your service standards well above the norm.

It sounds so simple, doesn't it? Well it is and it isn't. Outstanding service is a blend of attitude, systems and constant attention. It's more than just smiles and handshakes, it's a way of life. It requires a total commitment to the customer all the way through the business, not just words on a wall.

So, in order to help you deliver record-breaking, champion service, here are 13 (THE **LUCKY** 13) vital action points which should be ingrained into your company's operations and culture:

1. MOTIVATE YOUR CUSTOMERS TO TALK TO YOU BECAUSE SOUTH AFRICAN CUSTOMERS DO NOT COMPLAIN - THEY JUST DO NOT COME BACK!

In the USA only 1 out of 27 unsatisfied customers complain. So, imagine what the ratio is in South Africa. *The Golden Secret, though, is that if you handle the complaint correctly, 95% of your unhappy customers will return as your most loyal customers.* Here's your challenge: You have to proactively identify your dissatisfied customers and give them a way to complain in a user friendly, simple manner.

When customers are asked why they do not complain they say:
- How do I complain?
- It's not worth the time and effort
- People just don't care
- We are intimidated, afraid to complain

So make it easy for your customers to complain. In fact, give them an incentive to complain. Make them feel like it's their right to complain. Call them at random. Go looking for problems. Follow up, follow up, follow up. Customers who complain are more beneficial to your business than any expensive management consultant. The feedback you receive will be an invaluable tool in developing your product or service. Here are some feedback mechanisms you can consider:

- Create a customer care line or a 0800 number. If you do set up a call centre, make sure that it is manned properly. Nothing is more frustrating than a customer care line that is constantly engaged or that keeps customers on hold for twenty minutes. There are many companies that can help you set up this facility.
- Make rating cards available in your store or in your package with pre-paid postage and your address on the back. Give these cards

a catchy name like "What's the Score" or "Are we winning with you?"or as Nando's asks "Did we make a cluck-up?". Train your staff to encourage feedback from customers.

- Phone customers at random and check their satisfaction levels. This kind of action can lead to great word-of-mouth advertising, especially if you make the call yourself. So do it! Nothing impresses customers more than being called by the boss (that's you, remember?)
- Receive regular feedback from customers' complaints and keep track of how they are being handled e.g. the number of complaints, how were they handled, how quickly they were resolved, and what the results were - i.e. how many customers did repeat business with you.
- Celebrate your staff who handle customer complaints well. And make it easy for them to make the customer happy - i.e. Don't be cheap when it comes to making it right for the customer.

Note: There are some very good Customer Care Monitoring software packages available.

The bottom line is that the number of customer complaints received by your company is not an indication of how weak your business is, but how healthy. In business, no news is very bad news indeed.

2. SET YOUR CUSTOMER SERVICE RULES AND THEN IMPLEMENT THEM RELIGIOUSLY – DESIGN AND EXECUTE THE SERVICE PLAN.

There is an old business saying: Everyone knows what to do, but not everyone does what they know. The basic rule of customer service is very simple: *Do whatever it takes to make and keep customers so happy they come back for more again and again.* Not difficult is it? We'll tell you where the difficulty arises: executing that rule with passion, discipline and consistency.

How many companies do you know who provided magnificent service when they started and then faded into mediocrity? Stand guard against this danger destroying your business. Make customer service your personal mission. Drive customer service from the top, but always discuss and encourage your staff to be open about it so that everyone can turn around dissatisfied customers.

Customer Service is such an important part of your business that we recommend developing a service plan that forms an integral part of every sale. This plan could include action points such as offering a customer satisfaction guarantee with every sale or service; or it could include a no-questions asked exchange policy; or it could feature a range of personalised touches designed to fit the customer's tastes; or it could entail phoning the customer within 24 hours of the purchase, then again after three weeks and again after three months. For such a plan, it is vital to capture the contact details of every customer. This database will also become an invaluable marketing tool - it will empower you to build a deep and enduring relationship with the customer over time.

3. GREAT CUSTOMER SERVICE IS ABOUT HAVING THE GUTS TO FACE YOUR CUSTOMERS

How many company directors are prepared to release their home or cellphone numbers? How many of these directors phone or visit customers who have complained? We promise you that customers hate one thing above all else and that's being given the run-around by staff who have no authority to remedy a situation.

Most businesspeople try and avoid confrontations. They are scared to deal directly with a customer who "can't get no satisfaction". That's because they see the situation as a negative one. But what happens if you see every interaction with the customer as an opportunity to take your business to the next level? You'll search for ways to go eyeball-to-eyeball with your customers.

So make a commitment right now to always face a customer directly and not hide behind your frontline people.

4. DON'T RAISE FALSE EXPECTATIONS - DELIVER ON YOUR PROMISES, OR DIE TRYING.

Company A promises delivery at 2.00 p.m. but delivers at 3.00 p.m. Company B promises delivery at 4.00 p.m. and delivers at 3.00 p.m. Which company will you be most satisfied with? Be wary of committing to high service standards if there is even a remote possibility that you won't be able to deliver on them.

One of the biggest mistakes made by so many South African companies is their habit of over-promising and under-delivering. Very few things will kill your business faster than broken promises to customers. So, if you are going to make a big promise to a customer, make sure you deliver on it. If you do, you'll be a hero. If you don't, you'll be an outcast. There's no in between. And there's no going back. Once you lose a customer's trust, it's almost impossible to get it back again.

5. SERVICE IS A KEY PART OF THE QUALITY PERCEPTION. DON'T CUT BACK ON SERVICE TO REDUCE PRICE. CUSTOMERS WILL PAY A LITTLE BIT MORE FOR GREAT SERVICE.

"Many Marketers haven't got the guts to charge a lot of money for a really good product or service" – David Ogilvy.

Clever entrepreneurs have realised that customers are prepared to pay a premium for good service and convenience. They add value to their product or service by doing it better, faster, closer, and smarter than their competition. They know that there are two kinds of customers:

The first kind of customer values quality service. This kind of customer knows that there is no substitute for first class service delivery. This is the kind of customer who makes businesses successful. This is the kind of customer you want.

The second kind of customer is the kind of customer who just wants the "deal". They are purely price driven. They don't care that much about quality. They will make your life a misery. You can still make a living out of them but it will be tough, tough, tough.

What kind of customer do you want? It's your call. Make it now! We promise you - extraordinary service makes price less important in the eyes of the consumer.

6. SERVICE IS ABOUT PEOPLE: HIRE THE ATTITUDE, PROVIDE THE SKILLS

If you want to offer your customers 5-Star service, look for the desire to please others in the people you hire. Here's a fact: you cannot change people's attitudes if they do not want to change. If you hire people who do not have a genuine love of others, you'll never give it to them. And you will be stuck with non-performing employees who try drag everyone else down with them. The wrong people won't deliver the right service.

On the other hand, we believe in hiring potential champions and turning them into real ones. Once you've hired the "Right Stuff", then train them well. Give them the skills both through formal and on-the-job training. Ensure they thoroughly understand your company's mission and values. And give them the authority and responsibility to perform extraordinary acts of service excellence. Once again, we can't overemphasize its importance, recognise and reward great service lavishly. This is the one area of your business that will pay out immediately. And the best thing of all - it requires very little capital expenditure. If your people hire out their hearts, your customers' minds will follow.

7. LISTEN TO YOUR STAFF, TALK TO THEM AND, SOMETIMES, DO WHATEVER THEY SAY

One of your advantages as a small businessperson is that you will be very close to frontline staff. You will be able to talk to them, encourage them, motivate them, inspire them and learn from them.

That's right - make your frontline staff your customer service advisors. After all, they are the ones who interact with your customers everyday. We promise you that turned-on frontline staff will be a massive competitive advantage. They will be full of great ideas to serve your customers well. You just have to give them a chance to let these issues out. So plan weekly "Customer Service Pleasing Sessions". Just one day a week, open your business an hour later and get your people's opinions. And, once again, reward and recognise with abundance.

8. TEACH YOUR CUSTOMERS HOW TO BE GREAT CUSTOMERS:

In many instances, customers may not know how to buy correctly from you. Or they not know how to get the most from your business. One of the biggest favours you can ever do for your customers is train them how to maximise the benefit they get out of you. Very few companies take the time to teach their customers. The few that do are the few that are succeeding at the expense of their competition.

9. GRAB EVERY OPPORTUNITY TO LET YOUR CUSTOMERS KNOW HOW MUCH YOU ARE DOING FOR THEM BEHIND THE SCENES

Customers do not know what goes on behind the scenes. They take it for granted that everything will go the way they want it to go. Even when you go above and beyond the call of duty for them, they may not know how much effort you invested in meeting their needs. *So tell them.* But don't tell them in a boastful way. Just let them know the lengths to which your company will go to keep them happy. You'll be amazed at the positive response you'll receive.

10. IF YOU WANT OUTSTANDING SERVICE, YOU MUST MEASURE AND MONITOR ITS DELIVERY CONSTANTLY!

Service can be measured. There are a range of simple systems and yardsticks by which you can track your progress in this vital area. In fact, if you don't pay scrupulous attention to the measurement of your service delivery, you won't deliver great service. Period. What doesn't get measured, doesn't get done. So think about your business and the benchmarks for service excellence in your industry. Is it returns? Is it repeat purchases by customers? Is it the number of times a product comes in for repairs? Is it customer performance evaluations? Is it the cleanliness and hygiene of your store? Is it the quality of your displays? Is it the number of smiles on your customers' faces? Is it regular surveys that track your performance versus the competition? Is it turnaround time or customer waiting time? Whatever it is, *identify the most important benefits desired by your customers and measure how well you deliver these benefits to them.*

11. MAKE IT FUN, MAKE IT URGENT, MAKE IT A CHALLENGE!!

Customer service winners love to compete. They love the excitement that comes with a challenge. And they love the prizes that come with victory. So how can you implement fun customer service competitions within your company? How can you motivate your people to go the extra inch in delighting your customers? What targets can you set them that are ambitious but achievable? And what prizes can you give your people for outstanding performance?

Honour your Stars. Have regular ceremonies where awards are handed out and exceptional performance is recognised. From the very beginning, create a culture of celebration within your company. Ensure that your own people encourage each other to perform. So don't just have awards for the Number One performers. Establish group incentives where everyone wins if company targets are achieved.

12. CULTIVATE ONE OF YOUR MOST POWERFUL ALLIES IN THE DELIVERY OF SUPERB CUSTOMER SERVICE: YOUR SUPPLIERS (OR REALLY YOUR EXTERNAL PARTNERS)

Your suppliers can be a powerful ally in the quest for exceptional customer service. In fact, they shouldn't even be called suppliers - they should be called your external partners.

As you plan your business, identify those external partners who are the best of the breed. Pinpoint those companies who are recognised as the leaders in their fields. And then romance them the way you would romance your customers. Invest as much time and effort as it takes to get close to your external partners. Treat them extremely well. Pay them on time. Let them know what's happening in your business. Recommend them to others. Involve them in your business. Invite them over for drinks. Buy them lunch. Get their ideas for improving your business.

You will be amazed by how much you can learn from them. After all, they have probably been in the industry for some time and they are probably supplying your competitors as well. So they understand the dynamics of your marketplace. What's more, because they want your business, they will probably be willing to share a lot of their information with you. Your external partners can be a goldmine of information on trends, competitive activity and new business opportunities. Use them.

There is another reason why you need to get close to your external partners. If they are the best in the industry, they are probably operating at or near maximum capacity. There will be times when they have to choose between serving you and serving your competitors. You want your external partners to decide in your favour because you have created such a loyal relationship with them.

13. SOMETIMES, AS A LAST RESORT, YOU HAVE TO FIRE YOUR CUSTOMERS.

Yes, we know it sounds crazy. Fire my customers? Yup. There are certain customers who will destroy your business. They want more and more for less and less. They are abusive to you and your staff. They don't pay on time. They don't respect your right to make a profit. These are the customers from hell. These are the customers you need to get rid of pronto.

But make sure you don't confuse demanding customers with customers from hell. You will have certain customers who demand their pound of flesh from you. They will push you hard to get maximum value for their Rand. These kind of customers can make you a better business. They will stretch you. They will help you perform better and faster.

So be very careful. But as a last resort - take the drastic step and walk away from the customers who are damaging your business.

THE BOTTOM LINE – OUR GUARANTEE TO YOU

We guarantee you that if your business delivers soul-stirring, mind blowing service, your business will thrive. You will be able to charge a price premium. Your customers will become your Raving Fans. Your staff will be happy and motivated. And you will become rich, famous and fulfilled.

But the bucks start here: Spectacular Customer service must become an obsession in your company from day one. You cannot afford to slack off even for an hour. You have to adopt a zero-excuse approach to consistently delighting your customers. Ready? Get Set. Go!

Part Three:

Franchising:
The Alternative Route to Riches

How to use other people's experience and
expertise to make it happen for yourself

"Franchising: The alternative option"

As you head into the third and final section of this book, you may still be wondering about what kind of business you actually want to launch. You may have the fire in your belly. You may be in The High-Performance Zone. You may have spent hours thinking about a business plan. But you may still be uncertain about where to go from here. Well, this session on Franchising may be just what you're looking for.

Globally, Franchising growth has been explosive. In South Africa, it is really just beginning

America has really fueled the explosive growth in franchising. In fact, in America franchising accounts for ± 42% of all retail business and ± 10% of the gross national product. In America, six million people are involved in half a million franchise outlets. In Australia, on the other hand, franchising accounts for 25% of all retail business. This is less than America but still much greater than South Africa.

In South Africa the growth in franchising has been slow mainly because the country has been dominated by a small number of large corporations. These companies tended to use their power to neutralize small businesses that appeared to be a possible threat. The fact that these large corporations have been forced to downsize and unbundle has been a great stimulation for the growth of small business - led by franchising.

In South Africa, franchising accounts for only 9% of all retail business. However this figure is forecasted to escalate rapidly over the next 5 years. In fact, by 2004, we believe we will be close to the Australian figure of 25% - that's a growth of almost 200%. So, if you are reading this section now, you are about to get into a part of South African economy that's going to take off like a rocket. Fasten your seatbelts.

We estimate that South Africa currently has over 400 franchisors. However, over half of these franchisors are not members of the Franchise Association of Southern Africa ("F.A.S.A"). It is our opinion that because of F.A.S.A's high rating in the South African business community, all reputable franchisors should automatically become members of the association.

So right up front, we want to warn you: If a franchisor is not a member of F.A.S.A - STAY AWAY. Franchising with the right partner can help you make lots of money. Franchising with the wrong partner is a one-way ticket to the poorhouse.

90% of all new franchisees of reputable franchises succeed compared with about 20% of independent businesses.

90% of all new franchisees of reputable franchises succeed because their business conceptualizing and pre-planning has been done for them. Furthermore, Professor John Stanworth, director of the small business unit of the Polytechnic of Central London, has carried out extensive research into the motivation of those wishing to become franchisees. He states that, "it is quite possible that as many as 50% of franchisees would not otherwise have become self employed, if it was not for the franchise format". This factor shows the power of franchising and the exciting opportunities for those who become involved in this dynamic sector.

So what is franchising? It means "being in business for yourself but not by yourself"

The word "franchise" comes from the French language and means privilege or freedom. In this sense, franchising offers people the freedom to own, manage and direct their own business. It means "being in business for yourself but not by yourself" according to Nic Louw, executive director of FASA quoted from the 1999 Franchise Book of Southern Africa.

Franchising is a collaboration between an independent person and a company that wishes to expand its business. This collaboration is governed by a franchise agreement. In order to expand its business the company (franchisor) allows a third party (franchisee) the right to use its trade name, business methods and know-how. In return, the franchisee, who is an independent trader, accepts certain restrictions on the way he or she conducts their business. The franchisee also agrees to make royalty payments to the franchisor. This type of franchising is often referred to as Business Format Franchising.

The term franchising is often used out of context and results in confusion between other agreements such as distributorships, agency agreements and licensing agreements.

Distributorships occur where a third party acquires goods on his account from a supplier for on-sale to customers. Such agreements will not usually require the distributor to trade under a specified name or put restrictions on the way he should run his business. The supplier's return will be obtained in the mark up he charges the distributor. The distribution agreement will contain some restriction on the distributor relating to products to be supplied e.g. minimum quantities, servicing, guarantees etc.

Agency agreements are similar to distributorships except that the agent does not purchase products from the supplier but on-sells the products on behalf of the supplier, while charging the supplier a commission for his services.

Licensing agreements also contain some elements which are found in franchising agreements, namely the licensing of know-how, or intellectual property rights, but are usually more associated with manufacturing than marketing and seldom contain restrictions in the way that the licensee can operate his business.

Advantages of franchising for franchisees

1. *The franchisee will start a tried and tested business concept that has been fully "pilot" tested.* Often franchisees do not have the general business management skills or specialised knowledge needed in the proposed business activity. The franchisor owns this knowledge and has the necessary business skills, which he passes on to the franchisee.

2. *The franchisor should have developed a long-term strategic business plan including a country development plan, which the franchisee will be exposed to.* The franchisor's strategic vision should provide for the growth and adaptability required for the survival of the brand. A country development plan is the geographic expansion plan that outlines the geographic areas earmarked for expansion, as well as the rate of expansion. The rollout of the franchisee's store is therefore part of a larger expansion strategy, so the brand that the franchisee has bought into should become more valuable with time.

3. *The franchisor should use scientific site selection criteria and give the franchisee a well-calculated, protected trade area around his business.* Ideally, the country development plan should be based on a well-developed expansion strategy that incorporates the geographic requirements for the sustainability of a site, e.g. number of households or number of economically active people. This scientific site selection should ensure that each franchisee will have a viable business in his/her area.

4. *As a franchisee, you will be the owner of your own business; however, restrictions will be imposed on you by the franchise agreement.* These restrictions usually include prescriptions on the use of trademarks, marketing campaigns and standards of operating. By abiding by these prescriptions and specified standards, the risks of business failure are substantially reduced.

5. *The franchisee will be able to make use of the franchisor's purchasing power and other benefits relating to the size of the operation* e.g.
• The franchisee should set up the business at a lower cost. The franchisor should be able to source capital equipment and shopfitting at lower prices because of bulk buying and relationships with suppliers.
• The franchisee should find it easier to raise capital. An established franchise usually has a strong brand and goodwill, which will influence a banker's decision when granting the franchisee a loan.
• The franchisee should be able to purchase goods on an ongoing basis at preferable prices. Again, this is due to the franchisor's ability to buy in bulk and good supplier relations.
• The franchisee should be offered participation in the franchisor's medical aid, provident fund etc. These are benefits that an independent business may not be able to obtain at the same preferential rates.

6. *The franchisor should provide its franchisees with both initial and ongoing training both on a theoretical and practical level.* The franchisor's support staff provides "on-the-job" training when visiting the site, while the franchisor should organize special courses and seminars for the franchisees and staff alike.

7. *The franchisee should benefit from the franchisor's ongoing new product and concept development.* The franchisor has the infrastructure in place to support a research and development function within the operation, or the resources to outsource this function. New product/concept development is vital for the survival of a product. However, franchisees should also be able to provide their input into product/service development. Numerous new products introduced into McDonalds started as franchisees' ideas.

8. *The franchisee can take advantage of the brand name and reputation that has been developed by the franchisor.* This may reduce the lead-time in making a business successful and may even reduce the amount of working capital required.

9. *The franchisee will receive the use of proven systems and controls.* This includes Point Of Sale systems specifically designed for the concept and customized accounting packages.

10. *The franchisee will tap into the franchisor's tried and tested price strategy and costing systems.* The franchisor can experiment with pricing strategies in a controlled way, e.g. by testing new prices at selected company owned stores first.

11. *The franchisee will receive an updated, workable operations manual, which will help him/her to run the business in all aspects* e.g. registering the business, marketing, labour laws, production standards etc. The operations manual is the blueprint for running the business and must get updated regularly.

12. *The franchisee should receive regular communication and motivation from the franchisor.* The franchisor should organize an annual franchisee conference as well as other communication initiatives to keep franchisees aware of industry trends, operational decisions and marketing initiatives.

13. *The franchisee will have a successful, proven asset to sell when deciding to move on.* The value of the brand and the goodwill accumulated will contribute to this.

Disadvantages of franchising for a franchisee

1. *A franchisee is subject to substantial control by the franchisor.* The franchisor has to ensure that a range of operating standards must be adhered to. These restrictions are obviously absent in independent businesses. It therefore takes a special kind of entrepreneur to become a franchisee. The kind of entrepreneur who makes a successful franchisee is willing to work hard, provide his own input and, most importantly, operate within the prescribed parameters of the franchisor.

2. *A franchisee pays an upfront fee and ongoing royalties.* This upfront fee can be substantial. The franchisee may therefor need to incur a heavy debt load to start the business. Although these fees and royalties help the franchisor in building the brand and supporting the franchisee, they can lead to an adversarial relationship between franchisor and franchisee.

3. *There may be restrictions on the franchisee's ability to sell the business.* The franchisor will normally have first option to purchase the business or approve the potential buyer. This may slow down the selling process and impact the selling price.

4. *The success of the franchise operation and the franchisee's business is heavily dependent on the ability of the franchisor and the other franchisees.* To a large extent, therefor, the well being of the franchisee is directly related to the sustained vision and performance not just of the franchisor but also of the other franchisees. It only takes a few bad franchisees to kill the brand in the eyes of the consumer. That's because the consumer perceives all outlets of a franchise as being part of one organization. So, once again, buyer beware!!

Investing in a franchise: Take it slow. This is your life we're talking about here

Take great care before investing in a franchise. Under no circumstance should you be rushed into taking up a franchise. This is your life we're talking about here.

Firstly, you must evaluate your own skills, aptitude and abilities.

Based on the pros and cons of being a franchisee outlined in the previous section, decide whether you will be a good franchisee. Taking up a franchise will impose substantial burdens on both you and your family. You will be required to invest large sums of your time and money (or even borrowed money) in the franchise.

Secondly, establish the areas of business activities that you are interested in. Obtain lists of available franchisees. F.A.S.A will let you have a list of its members – phone them (011) 484-1285/8 and unless exceptional circumstances prevail, deal only with F.A.S.A. members.

Thirdly, obtain details of those franchisors that are in your area of interest. Compare their terms, track records, reputation and size. Narrow your choice down to three or four.

Fourthly, really do your homework on your short list. The types of questions you should ask your potential franchisor include: -

- Is there a demand in the market for the products / services? The market demand must be sizeable, sustainable and substantiated with legitimate sales and marketing statistics.
- Has the product / service got staying power? A fad cannot be franchised, since it doesn't have long term potential.
- What is the track record of the franchisor? If franchisees are selling out at an alarming rate or if your bank is not impressed when mentioning the franchisor's name, you should be cautious. A good franchisor has excellent references, happy franchisees and a good reputation in its specific industry.
- How many franchisors are in existence in this industry and what profits are they making? Make sure that your franchisor of choice is measuring up to industry standards and benchmarks.
- Does the franchisor have a solid, experienced management team? Support is vital to a franchisee and should be provided by competent, knowledgeable support staff.
- Who is the competition and how strong are they? Make sure that your prospective franchisor has a sizeable slice of the cake.
- Speak to potential banks and see if the bank approves the franchisor. If they don't, chances are that you will have difficulty in obtaining financing.

- Ask for and ensure you obtain an updated "disclosure document" which will give you full details about the franchisor concept and its directors. All FASA members are required to provide potential franchisees with a disclosure document.
- Go and visit a selection of franchisees and establish if they are happy with their investment.
- How efficiently did they handle your enquiry about a franchise? If you experienced unexplained delays or any confusion at head office level, chances are that you are not dealing with a competent organization. Things could only get worse.
- Is the franchisor choosy about the sort of people it accepts as franchisees? This is important, since the calibre of franchisees within the group will determine the reputation and ultimately, the performance of the franchise.
- Finally, is the franchisor prepared to show you the financial results of his company owned pilot stores? Are these stores performing well?

You should not be embarrassed about asking these questions. You and your family's future is at stake. So if a prospective franchisor makes you feel uncomfortable, or indicates that he is in a position to sell the franchise to persons less difficult than you, steer clear. There are many other great opportunities out there.

Finally franchisors normally fall into one of the following categories: -

1. Excellent and established professional franchisor.
2. Franchisor of a promising but unproven concept.
3. Rip off artist doomed for failure due to lack of experience and untried concept.

It is essential that you avoid the third category. You should not necessarily be daunted by category two, provided that you are aware that you are taking on a speculative venture and that the risk is high. We would not recommend the second category until the concept has been piloted for at least one year.

If you've got the right stuff as a franchisee of a franchise in category one, you are ready for a successful and happy future. Yes, there is hard work ahead of you. But we know you're ready for that challenge. By this stage of the book, you know how to motivate yourself and you understand how to start and manage a business. What's holding you back? Make it happen. And let us share in your success. E-mail us on lipkin@global.co.za.

Before you leap, know thyself via the ee test

You can start off with a big advantage if you can truly say that you know yourself well in terms of the various qualities and skills needed to run a successful business. Well, the ee test is an application of a tool called SPEEX(situation specific evaluation expert). This tool was designed, developed and tested in South Africa for South Africans. Originally normed on over 19 000 South Africans, this is the only tool that can genuinely be considered to be culturally fair for assessing individuals in the South African workplace.

Most other tests measure aspects of personality. While they may give you accurate personality profiles, what they don't give you is a measurement of your abilities, skills and potential in terms of what's needed to succeed in your own business. If you are interested in finding out more about the ee test, call Omnicon Recruitment on (011) 483-3163.

To help you on your way, here are seventeen of South Africa's Best:

Over the years, Eric has worked and mixed with many franchisors and service providers. Only a few have stood the test of time, professionalism and quality. We have invited seventeen of South Africa's Best to participate in this book and share with you the opportunities they offer.

The Franchise opportunities and service providers on the following pages are drawn from a range of industries. We believe they are all "Class Acts". Consider the possibilities they provide. Follow up. Be cautious. Be thorough. Be true to yourself. Be decisive.

The companies represented on the following pages include (in alphabetical order) ABSA, Baby Boom, Butterfield Bread, Debonairs Pizza, DM Kisch Inc, King Pie, Kleins, Liberty Life, Nando's, Nizams, Multiserv, PG Autoglass, Pick 'n Pay Franchise, Pleasure Foods, Postnet, Spec-Savers and Spur Steak Ranches.

Go make it happen!!

ABSA - SMOOTHING THE PATH TO SUCCESS

If you make one solid partnership and friendship in your quest to be your own boss and become rich, then it has to be with your bank.

You either love them or hate them! But you can't do without them! Banks seem to dominate your every move ... can't even get that Ferrari because they won't lend me the money ... can't go to Mauritius, got no money! To turn my dreams into reality, I'll need money, money, money!

True as that might be, there are ways and means of overcoming that gigantic problem with a capital G! First off, don't panic ... don't give up! Most millionaires started with nothing, put their life and belongings on the line; took the risk and lived to tell the tale as they sit on a tropical beach in Hawaii!

You've read the book, you're fired up! You've chanted those three magic words ... "I'm the Boss" and you're rearing to go! You've taken those first steps to turn your dream into reality. You've had that brilliant idea, researched the market, checked out the competition, put together a Business Plan, counted your cents - and horror of horrors! you don't have enough cash!

What you mustn't do is go off on a tangent about how banks are all the same - they take your money but will not loan you any. Remember, the more positive and excited you are about the project, the more chance you have of influencing the bank to loan you the money. The other thing is you must be fully prepared. If you walk into the bank manager's office and simply demand a loan without having done your homework, you're as good as dead. Be prepared ... be positive ... be pro-active.

Pro-active is the term that best describes *ABSA's* Franchise Desk and New Enterprise Banking unit. At long last, banks have come into line with the political and economic trend geared towards small business and more importantly they have recognised the potential of the entrepreneur. Working in tandem with the Governments' national initiative to support the Small and Medium Enterprises (SME), most banks and in particular *ABSA*, support these initiatives and have come a long way in assisting and coping with the new emerging entrepreneur.

Crucial alliances have been forged with Khula Credit Guarantee to facilitate the provision of guarantees to entrepreneurs requiring new enterprise finance but who do not meet the banks' minimum qualifying criteria. In these instances Khula will guarantee a percentage of *ABSA's* unsecured portion of loans that do qualify for the scheme. In addition to re-structuring a new approach to servicing the small operator, *ABSA* already has the capacity to grant finance nation-wide to new enterprises.

So, you've made it into the Bank Manager's office - smiles and all! Now what? According to *ABSA*, question number one is: Are you the owner-operator of the business? Score 1. Are you fully prepared? Score 2. Present them with a proper Business Plan and a realistic cash flow statement and you've scored more. Got a clean record? And by that we mean both legal and financial. Pass go and collect another brownie point.

In *ABSA's* case, their Franchise Desk has often helped Franchisees get onto their feet by loaning them the money to start their franchise business with a tailor made financial solution. Looking with pride at how the franchise operations they have financed have blossomed and grown, the bank is only too pleased to assist those prospective Franchisees who would like to purchase an existing franchise operation or start a new one.

Banks have to minimise their risks and *ABSA* is no exception. Franchising presents one of the safest forms of business in the market. A survey done by the US Commerce Department traced the success of 100 independently owned businesses and 100 franchises over a 10 year period. At the end of the first year, 97 franchises were still in operation compared with 62 independent businesses. By the 10th year, 90 franchises were going strong, but only 18 independent businesses had survived. With stats like these, no wonder banks are backing the winning horse - franchising.

The prospect for small business support is looking good. According to Philip Vosloo, Senior Manager, Business Market, "Loans are readily available to people who have a good Business Plan, are good operators and have some money of their own and are prepared to put themselves on the line."

ABSA - IN THE FOREFRONT OF BUSINESS START-UPS!

ABSA FRANCHISE DESK
Philip Vosloo   (011)350-5478
Riaan Fouchè   (011)350-5780
Christo Weideman (011)350-5704

ABSA NEW ENTERPRISE BANKING
Dawn Jefferson-Green (011) 350-4741/4881

BABY BOOM . . . INSTINCTIVELY THE RIGHT CHOICE

Judging by the *Baby Boom* payoff line this is a franchise opportunity that could well be the right choice.

*The distinct personal feeling that one gets on a visit to a **Baby Boom** store as well as the impressive range of products is reason enough to believe that this niche baby operation is going to be around for some time to come.*

The secret to investing in a franchise concept is to find a concept that is going to stand the test of time. The ***Baby Boom*** business format franchise is that of a baby store that offers a wide range of specialised baby goods in order for the customer to have an enjoyable shopping experience in a "one stop baby shop". After all, there will always be plenty of babies needing baby products and nappies.

Illona Duke and a partner started their ***Baby Boom*** concept from their homes in 1991 selling that most basic of baby items - the disposable nappy. The home based nappy business grew to such an extent that in 1992 the first ***Baby Boom*** store was opened in Glenhazel, Johannesburg and proved a huge success with sales of disposable nappies soaring and soon other baby accessories were added to the retail range.

So successful was the first store that the owners decided to have their own house brand of nappy manufactured and licenced and so the ***Baby Boom*** Disposable Nappy was born - the first and the core product of a long line of baby products which today make up the Baby Boom brand. ***Baby Boom*** have worked hard on their concept since that first venture and today there are close to 20 Baby Boom stores around the country - from Table View to Nelspruit, from Witbank to Upington.

Following the international trend of "speciality" stores, ***Baby Boom*** very quickly found its niche in the South African market. Designed as a one-stop destination store, ***Baby Boom*** customers will make a specific journey to patronise the store and the franchise enjoys strong brand loyalty. The extensive marketing of ***Baby Boom*** created significant brand awareness countrywide. Thus when a new ***Baby Boom*** store opens, the brand is generally well received by the local community.

Having developed brand loyalty from their customers with the disposable nappy brand which has become a household name, ***Baby Boom*** then introduced a whole range of branded products - from prams, campcots, walking rings, wet wipes, breast pads etc, all manufactured by the leading international manufacturers to the highest quality and safety standards.

The business requires a very special team to operate the franchise and very special franchisees to build the brand and provide the required service levels. This has been achieved through a philosophy and culture of caring that permeates throughout the group as well as a strong emphasis on empowering joint venture partners and staff through seminars and training.

Baby Boom is a family owned business run jointly by the Duke and Helberg families. The two families are fully involved in all aspects of the business on a day to day basis and have developed a range of skills unparalleled in the baby industry.

Baby Boom stores operate on several ownership levels combining company owned, joint venture and 100% franchisee owned stores. This unique franchise structure works extremely well for the group as *Baby Boom* have used mainly company owned stores to develop and refine their concept.

– *Baby Boom* offers two franchise options:
  The *Baby Boom* Joint Venture Store is a joint venture between the franchisor who holds 51% and the incoming franchisee who holds 49%. A minimum capital outlay of R300,0000 is required depending on the size of the outlet. These joint venture stores will be situated in larger metropolitan areas only.

– The *Baby Boom* "Country Store" is more in the line of a convenience store/baby boutique and will comprise mainly "destination" type stores in smaller towns. The franchisee owns 100% of the franchise and a minimum capital of R150,000 is required to finance the business.

The franchisee selection process is quite rigid as the nature of the business calls for a very special kind of person who has great empathy with customers and who will understand the "baby" market as well as run their own business with passion. In addition to the extensive training given by head office, a prospective franchisee must work for a period of time in a *Baby Boom* store to familiarise themselves on all aspects of the business and get a feel for the baby market. If you feel *Baby Boom* is the right business for you contact:

Jacob Helberg
Development Director, *Baby Boom*
Tel No: (011) 974-1316   Fax No: (011) 974-1614   Cell No: (082) 370-9351

... INSTINCTIVELY THE RIGHT CHOICE

BUTTERFIELD BREAD - FEEDING THE NATION

Bread feeds a nation... and Butterfields caters to the needs of the masses!

In a country like South Africa, where some nine million loaves of bread are consumed every day, it makes sense to invest in a **Butterfield Bread** franchise.   The opportunity to reach all sectors of the population with freshly baked, wholesome bread at an affordable price is one of the unique aspects of this franchise which started in Pretoria in 1996 and which by the end of 2000 will have in excess of 150 stores nationwide. At present, **Butterfield Bread** is opening a bakery every 120 hours and with all their operations running at full steam are still only baking two percent of the nine million loaves of bread consumed in SA every day.

"If that isn't one damn good reason to invest in **Butterfield Bread**," says Kobus Oosthuizen, the 33 year old Managing Director of **Butterfield Bread**, "than I don't know what is!" Bread has always been the basis of survival in our country. The old days saw mass subsidisation of bread... the lifting of government subsidies saw inflated prices being paid by the consumer due to the enormous overheads of the giant plant bakeries and the smaller bakeries not being able to penetrate all market sectors.   **Butterfield Bread** was conceived as the solution to the problem, capitalising on the limitations of existing bread baking institutions. Taking into account the fact that bread is by far the most important consumer commodity and widely accepted staple food of the nation, the stage is set for an almost guaranteed franchise concept in the Southern African retail and wholesale bread market. "The bottom line" says Kobus Oosthuizen, "is that large plant bakeries don't retail, and in store bakeries don't wholesale, so we thought it would be a good idea to position ourselves in the middle and scrape some of the cream from both sides!"

Franchising this unique concept remains the best tested operational structure in executing the **Butterfield Bread** business plan and brand building exercise. Excellent product quality and the highest operational standards underlies the concept of hourly, freshly baked wholesome bread through decentralised franchised bakeries. There is a worldwide trend towards the small convenience store concept and away from the bulk buying which extinguished traditional businesses of the local baker. There was once a time when every little town and village had its own bakery - where fresh, crisp rolls were baked throughout the day and where shoppers could purchase good wholesome bread at reasonable prices. **Butterfield Bread** is bringing back those good old days by franchising and rapidly expanding into every little town and suburb in South Africa.

A secret to the success of the **Butterfield Bread** concept is its open-plan store design, which allows customers to view the entire baking process, from basic preparation of mixing to moulding and baking. Although the bread production is the core of the brand, a range of confectionary including rolls, croissants, Chelsea Buns, scones, hot cross buns and doughnuts are on the menu and pizza slices take care of the lunch time trade. The concept lends itself to ongoing activity throughout the day and caters for breakfast, lunch and take-home trade.

The cost of a typical franchise is around R600,000 - of which about R450,000 is for equipment. Set-up costs include things such as opening stock, signage, electrical installations, plumbing and rental deposit. Franchisees are charged a variable monthly royalty calculated on total flour and pre-mix purchases. Every aspect of the *Butterfield Bread* franchise operation has been tried, tested and proven, from the supply of raw materials to the production process, and to the presentation and marketing of the brand.

Thorough training of franchisees and their staff remains key to *Butterfield Bread's* effective operation. Says Oosthuizen, "A potential franchisee need not be overly worried that he or she cannot actually bake bread. What we are more interested in is someone who has good administrative sense, personnel management skills, can plan well, and above all, is operationally involved. The latter, in fact, is non-negotiable: we won't take anyone that is not hands-on."

A well-received avenue for bread distribution within the Butterfield family is *Butterfield on Wheels*, which is a home delivery and wholesale distribution service that operates under a separate franchising system. Although operating within existing franchisee's territory, the *Butterfield on Wheels* concept delivers to residential areas, goes on to wholesale deliveries and then services high traffic areas throughout the day. This concept is ideal for the lower entry level entrepreneur who with an initial outlay of as little as R10,000 can get into business. Other opportunities for empowerment lie in the tailor-designed Butterfield pushcarts and trailers.

With its aim to be represented throughout the consumer line from low income earners through to South Africa's highest income earners, the *Butterfield Bread* franchise is certainly feeding a colourful nation!

BUTTERFIELD – THE BRAND IN BREAD!
BUTTERFIELD HOLDINGS (PTY) LTD
Tel: No: (012) 322-6144
Fax No: (012) 322-6149
e-mail: kobus@butter.co.za
Website: www.butter.co.za

DEBONAIRS PIZZA - THE TALK OF THE TOWN!

Dazzling . . . Dashing . . . Daring to be Different . . . that's Debonairs!

There is nothing more exciting than being the " hottest" new fast food concept - one that has a fresh new approach and a great vibe - that takes the country by storm! Well, **Debonairs Pizza** has done just that! Its black and white image and dashing style of its delivery personnel in bowties shouts "We've arrived!" and indeed they have. It's becoming a common sight to see **Debonairs Pizza's** elegant drivers in tuxedos delivering piping hot pizzas to your office or home, backed by the promise of R10 off the next order if their delivery time exceeds 45 minutes.

In 1997 **Debonairs Pizza** scooped the FASA's (Franchise Association of Southern Africa) Brand Builder of the Year Award and in 1998 won the prestigious Franchisor of the Year accolade. Not bad going for a franchise concept that was started in 1991 by two 23-year old Pietermaritzburg students, Craig Mackenzie and Andrew Harvey, who saw the gap in the franchise pizza market and opened the first exclusive pizza outlet in Pietermaritzburg that offered free delivery, discount for slow delivery service and smart tuxedo service.

With Andrew's experience, they set about creating a sophisticated data base, which turned out to be the key ingredient to the success of the franchise. Their marketing strategy of capturing customer data and bombarding them with promotional communications and personal service incentives was, unbeknown to them, the concept of "relationship marketing" that today is the buzzword in global communications. Their concept of free delivery pre-empted the trend towards family "home replacement meals" which is fast becoming an integral component of take-outs. In both instances **Debonairs Pizza** were right on the mark and ahead of the field!

Today **Debonairs Pizza** is a runaway success! Ranked amongst the top 10 food franchises in South Africa, it is the leading pizza brand with growth in excess of 203% per annum. With outlets opening at a rate of one every 8.5 days, **Debonairs Pizza** expects to have 120 stores by the start of the millennium. Sales are expected to top the R150 million mark by the end of 1999 and most stores achieve an average R1,800 sales per sq. metre each month.   The rapid expansion of the franchise has created investments totalling approximately R45 million and over 650 jobs.

Debonairs Pizza is a young and progressive company and with the partnership created with the Steers Group now has access to prime retail space, ongoing support and training in all aspects of franchise management.   Prospective franchisees are carefully screened and in keeping with their "dashing" image look for partners who have some entrepreneurial flair and who are looking for a better future for themselves.

Enthusiasm, hard work, the ability to communicate, honesty and because its a franchise, the discipline to work within someone else's plan are the characteristics that make for a successful *Debonairs Pizza* franchisee. Franchisees receive training in all facets of owning and running a franchise and are entitled to Steers Group buying benefits. Over a third of all new stores are owned by franchisees from previously disadvantaged communities and an impressive 23% of franchisees have become multiple store owners.

The financial requirements for a franchise is R250,000 in cash, for a full investment of approximately R530,000. Franchisees can expect to achieve gross margins of 60% - 65%. The average store turnover is in the region of R155,000 per month, with several stores doing more than R300,000 per month and all outlets notching up a 100% success rating. Sites for new outlets are carefully selected and over saturation is avoided by positioning outlets in one of the approximately 200 scientifically identified sites which promotes excellent returns for franchisees.

The expansion drive of Southern Africa's "smartest" food franchise has not been limited to South Africa. The *Debonairs Pizza* stores have appeared in Zimbabwe, Swaziland and Kenya and franchise opportunities exist in the Inland region, Eastern and Western Cape and throughout Africa.

Debonairs Pizza invites enthusiastic applicants to join Southern Africa's thriving home delivery powerhouse.

DEBONAIRS PIZZA MAKES IT EASY FOR FRANCHISES TO MAKE A WHOLE LOT OF DOUGH!

DEBONAIRS PIZZA
Tel No: (011) 315 3000
Fax No: (011) 315 0059

DM KISCH INC. - FRANCHISE LAW AND KNOW-HOW

Going into business for yourself and being your own boss - whether you intend starting your own mini-empire, starting a franchise or simply buying into a franchise can be the most important and exciting time of your life.

But . . . it can also be a minefield of legal entanglement if not handled properly by competent lawyers who have an in-depth understanding of the many facets of the franchising business. If, for example you have a business concept or structure you wish to franchise, you need to obtain sound legal advise on issues such as the type of business medium or licencing structures best suited to your needs; advice on the use and protection of the intellectual capital which the business possesses and/or will develop or acquire in the course of conducting its operations, examples being method of business software, trade secrets, trade marks, trade names, get up, designs, and a variety of material protectable under copyright law. If the business is more technologically orientated you will need advice on patents, know-how and functional designs – not only in regard to protection but also as to the on-going strategic management of such assets. At the outset it is imperative that the trade mark, company names and technology to be used in the franchise operation are available for use in the Republic or elsewhere, and that no intellectual property rights are being infringed.

Any new business would need legal assistance in commercial law matters – from close corporation registrations, company registrations and defensive company name registrations. Where more than one party contributes assets or capital to the venture, advice will be required on corporate structuring, acquisitions and mergers. *D.M.KISCH*, in addition to dealing with the standard legal set-up requirements, specialises in assisting franchisors in evaluating the intellectual property of the business with special emphasis on its strategic aims and objectives. To this end it conducts feasibility studies, devises business development strategies and advises on the selection of suitable franchise operations and the preparation of related documentation such as franchise agreements, disclosure documents and operations manuals; domain name registration and advice on doing business on the internet; the drafting of suitable employment contracts; and labour issues peculiar to franchising, including restraints of trade.

A franchise business usually *centres around* the empowering of individual franchisees, giving them a blueprint to success in a tried and tested business initiative that in most cases proves mutually beneficial to both parties. It is the nature of franchising to allow individuals with little direct experience to buy into a franchise concept and to receive training and assistance from the franchisor in establishing a successful business. It therefore relies heavily on contracts between the two parties, to balance the scales of what the franchisor is offering and what the franchisee is buying. The drawing up of a contract that is fair to both parties is another aspect of franchising that is crucial to the success of the business and which needs to be drawn up by a competent franchise lawyer.

Once up and running, a franchise's Intellectual Capital is never static: there is always continuous development and often intellectual capital management issues arise which require skill and insight if the business is to grow rather than degenerate into fruitless conflicts. Franchises change hands, legal problems arise with franchisees in breach of contract, contracts need renewing and suppliers' contracts need to be continually updated – all areas that are best tackled by lawyers with the requisite experience and acumen in such matters.

D.M. Kisch undertakes not only Trade Mark, Patent and Company Office searches and advice on availability, suitability and protection of the intellectual property that a franchise business wishes to use, but also devises structures for optimal utilisation of such intellectual capital for stock exchange listings, licencing and corporate finance purposes. A law firm can also be invaluable in assisting in the calculation of the appropriate sale price when the business is sold, or valued for corporate finance purposes - as there are a host of intellectual property issues which impact directly on the value that can be obtained from or for a business.

Established in 1874, *D.M. Kisch* has a long and distinguished history in the field of Intellectual Property Law. With offices in Sandton, Pretoria and St Helier Jersey, a support and professional staff complement of 130, including fifteen directors, it is positioned to advise local and international businesses and in particular franchisors and franchisees regarding the complexities of the local franchise market. In addition its network of agents and correspondents ensure that it is able to offer clients a professional service internationally.

D.M. Kisch holds the enviable position of legal advisors to FASA (The Franchise Association of Southern Africa) and have had considerable exposure to the governing provisions relating to the establishment and management of franchise operations, in particular the guidelines set by the Business Practices Committee, FASA and the Competition Board. They are involved in the implementation of the newly introduced Competition Act and are spearheading an investigation and representation on behalf of FASA on this important piece of legislation.

D.M. Kisch offers its clients a combination of skills, commitment and experience, ensuring sound legal advice and assistance in establishing and managing a business or franchise operation to the client's best commercial advantage.

TAKE APPROPRIATE ADVICE BEFORE EMBARKING ON A BUSINESS VENTURE OR FRANCHISE – INVEST IN ADVICE FROM A LAW FIRM WITH THE REQUISITE SKILL AND EXPERIENCE.

D.M. KISCH INC.
Tel No: (011) 884-8852/60   Fax No: (011) 884-8873/5

DMK
D.M.KISCH

KING PIE - A UNIQUELY SOUTH AFRICAN CONCEPT

King Pie is King of the pie-makers ... and offers you a giant slice of the pie!

The nineties was the decade of transformation ... in every respect! But possibly the most staggering turnaround in the fast food market was the re-birth of the pie! How many of you remember those bad old days when pies were bought from the local cafe and were somewhat suspect?

King Pie started in Pretoria in 1993 with a pilot operation that focused on offering a freshly baked range of pies made daily on the premises in full view of the public. The concept was a runaway success with people queuing to buy their favourite pie, knowing and seeing it was freshly made and baked. Within a year there were over 50 franchises and today *King Pie* boasts well over 300 outlets countrywide, selling approximately 8 million pies per month with a capital base of around R35 million. The freshly baked pie market as a whole is estimated at R500 million rand and is still considered to be in the growth stage. At an average R3.50 per pie, that's quite an achievement! Sceptics, both in franchising and business, thought the concept would not take off.... that it would fizzle out. "Who", they intoned, "could make money out of a R3.50 pie?" *King Pie's* reply to that was, "With 43 million South African's who love pies and above all who can afford to buy one of their range of fourteen ... there can be no question of success!

King Pie is without doubt the largest pie franchise in South Africa and is one of the fastest growing food franchises in the country. Fast food has become prohibitively expensive, with most brands only catering to the top end of the market and few of them offering take out items for under R5.00 ... or even R10.00! By franchising the concept and pioneering the concept of on-site preparation and baking, pies have now become an acceptable and welcome take-out item, and its appeal goes far beyond just the fast food category. With the world-wide move towards "home replacement meals", King Pie's Tasty Twelves and Six Mix have become popular with working families who can have a wholesome and hassle free meal. Research has shown that pies are the one food item that appeals to all sectors, and is the most affordable of all take-out food items.

Perhaps the most positive aspect of the burgeoning pie market has been the improvement in the quality of the pies and in this respect *King Pie* leads the field. The art of pie-making has become an exact science that ensures only the finest ingredients are used and consistent quality is maintained. *King Pie* controls the standards and production from the quality of the raw materials, with flour specified and only the best de-hydrogenised pastry fat used to the optimum weight and content of the filling with specified cube solids (meat content) resulting in a pie that measures up to highest standards as well as satisfies the customers' taste buds.

The *King Pie* franchisees come from all walks of life and it is not a pre-requisite to have any baking experience as all training, including all aspects of management, marketing and production are provided by the Holding Company. It will cost a prospective investor approximately R450,000 to set up a *King Pie* factory franchise. A smaller satellite Bake-Off costs in the region of R175,000. The container concept costs in the region of R95,000 and is aimed at areas without formal retail centres.

The average turnover of a *King Pie* factory franchise is in the region of R250,000 per month with return of capital at around 40%. *King Pie's* royalty structure differs from the standard norm in that royalties are pegged at a fixed rate depending on the size and type of outlet. The advantage in this system lies in the fact that, without the constraints of controlling and verifying exact turnover figures, the relationship between franchisor and franchisee is at its optimum best. The advertising contributions, which are determined at a percentage of the purchases, are administered completely separately by a national executive committee comprising representatives of the franchisor and regional franchisee representatives who determine the advertising strategy for the group.

King Pie recently became a member of the listed Rebhold Group which has interests in Liquor, Food, Freight, Beverages, Wholesale, Contract Catering and with the acquisition of *King Pie*, the retail sector. An injection of R5 million for store revamps has cemented *King Pie* as the largest pie franchise in Southern Africa. This has afforded *King Pie* the means necessary to become an even bigger force within the pie market. The strength of the *King Pie* brand increases constantly and is reinforced with a specialised operations team, innovative marketing and a top quality product.

KING PIE WILL GO DOWN IN HISTORY AS ONE OF THE MOST SPECTACULAR SUCCESS STORIES OF THE '90'S ... AND BEYOND!

KING PIE HOLDINGS
Tel No: (012) 46 3092
Fax No: (012) 346 1279
e-mail: intl@kingpie.co.za

KING🤴PIE

KLEINS - SET TO CAUSE A STIR IN FASHION ACCESSORIES

When an international franchise concept appears on the South African scene, there is great excitement. The very nature of franchising calls for new ideas, new concepts and fresh approaches. It also means that one is buying into a franchise company that has been operating successfully abroad and has a proven track record. What makes this new franchise concept to South Africa even more appealing is the fact that it is in the fashion accessory line – something quite unique and trendy! And, more importantly – it has no direct competitor in South Africa!

Kleins was founded in Australia in 1982 by Melbourne brothers Greg and Terry Campbell with the acquisition of 16 fashion accessory shops in the state of Victoria. Soon the *Kleins* concept could be found in every state and territory of Australia with 100 shops operating successfully. In 1990 the decision was taken to franchise the concept and further expansion into New Zealand and Fiji followed. Today, *Kleins* is the world's largest franchised fashion jewellery retailer with over 180 shops operating in the aforementioned countries.

As part of an ongoing commitment to international development a branch was registered in South Africa and a pilot scheme of four stores was established in selected Johannesburg shopping centres. Following the success of the pilot programme, a Master Franchise Agreement was finalised with entrepreneur Clive Knobbs who intends expanding into all corners of the country. A *Kleins* Franchised Store, under the master franchisee was introduced to the Kolonnade Centre in Pretoria in September 1998. It was an instant success with customers and has achieved trading densities at the upper level of South African expectations. There are presently five stores operating in Gauteng and several new stores are planned for the current year in all provinces.

The infrastructure of quality shopping centres throughout South Africa whose tennant mix includes a high proportion of fashion outlets is perfect for the introduction of *Kleins* into this retailing mix and presents a world-class shopping environment similar to that existing in Australia. Fashion accessories play an important role in the broader fashion sense and its appeal lies in the fact that, whilst new fashion trends can be expensive, a high fashion look can easily be achieved simply with the addition of good, affordable and high fashion accessories.

Kleins sell a wide range of Fashion Accessories designed to appeal to all age groups. The product range includes a range of quality fashion (costume) jewellery, house brand watches (exclusive to *Kleins*), ladies hats and hair accessories, scarves etc. Through its innovative approach to jewellery retailing *Kleins* has gained a well-deserved reputation for providing attractive quality merchandise at affordable prices. The Australian influence on *Kleins* will be reflected in terms of both value for money and excellence in customer service. Customers may join a frequent shopper club, entitling them to preferential discounts or other special offers.

A *Kleins* franchise investment costs between R190 000 and R240,000 including an up-front fee of R30,000. Management royalties are 15% with a 5% advertising contribution. An optimum store size, given adequate frontal exposure and configuration, is between 30 and 45 square metres, although premises outside this range may be considered in certain areas.

Kleins franchise owners receive detailed and extensive support from *Kleins*, to the extent that retail and fashion experience is not considered a pre-requisite to becoming a franchise owner. On-going training and in-store support is an integral part of the franchise programme with procedure manuals that cover the business and form the basis for ongoing training.

Kleins' marketing focus is on the use of aggressive promotional point-of-sale material. This provides strong visual impact at store level which is supported by a comprehensive program using various print and electronic media. The buying power of such a huge group as *Kleins* means that pricing is highly competitive and the latest trends in fashion will be filtered through from the overseas buyers who are *au fait* with the latest fashion trends in the international fashion jewellery and accessory industry.

Kleins have an international dedicated team of experienced retailers who will back the South African operation and will keep local franchisees abreast of product changes and management techniques. Their rapid expansion is recognised by the industry as a huge success in itself. Franchising a *Kleins* store makes good business sense: when you take into account the benefits you receive from the back up and resources of an international operation, you can see why the *Kleins* franchise option is so exciting!

KLEINS - LOOKING GOOD COSTS SO LITTLE

KLEINS
Tel No: (011) 455-4781
Fax No: 455-1078

Looking good costs so little

LIBERTY LIFE - TOP-OF-THE-LINE FRANCHISE

"Are you in the prime of your life - aged between 28 and 45 years - with a decade or more of managerial experience and an entrepreneurial spirit that says you should be getting into business for yourself? But . . . the thought of standing behind a counter serving beer or selling hamburgers and tackling labour problems just doesn't fit your profile and . . . well . . . it just isn't you and doesn't hold any appeal for you?

Consider this: Of the over 20 successful franchisees in the *Liberty Life New Venture Academy* since its launch in 1998, you'll find an airline pilot, a managing director of a property company, a clinical psychologist, a chemical engineer, mechanical engineer, a couple of CA's and LLB's. What do they all have in common? They, like millions of people around the world are discovering that life can present several challenges. The fact that you've trained in one discipline doesn't mean you can't be successful in another . . . and another! The world is changing so fast, yet through technology and communications is becoming more of a microcosm and people are grabbing opportunities to be successful with both hands. All it takes is that first step and you're away!

    Liberty Life believes that no matter what your background - if you've had long term managerial experience and business acumen, have perpetual enthusiasm and an entrepreneurial flair - then you're their man ... or woman! Following the franchising formula of "being in business for yourself, but not by yourself", the *Liberty Life* financial services franchise is one of the first of its kind for South Africa, a first in the financial services field and the first to offer a franchise concept .... with a difference!

    In the midst of the frenzy that is franchising today – with its big brands, hot new products and cool image, the *Liberty Life* financial services franchise is different in two respects:

One: It's a franchise with no royalties, no up-front fees and the franchisor will train you,finance you and establish you on the road of success in an independent business.

This win-win opportunity increases *Liberty Life's* potential to distribute its products and services; in turn the franchisee is helped to establish a viable, going concern by one of the most successful companies in South Africa's history.

Two: The *Liberty Life* New Venture Academy is raising the level of financial and business services to new heights by developing a franchise that fits snugly between the traditional tied-agency and a brokerage. The highly trained Liberty Life franchisees and consultants can now offer a new level of sophistication in investment and financial services. With so many financial options available to the public and with a buying market that is becoming more and more selective and discerning, the public are looking for more professional people to handle their financial affairs.

Pre-empting a huge shake-out in the market where only true professionals will survive, Liberty Life has been positioning itself to be the leader in the field. The company has spent millions of rands on the development of the Blueprint computer software, which enables the consultant to be actuarially sound in advising a client according to his needs, resources and risk profile. Wide knowledge is required to match the number of private and corporate investment products available today, from life assurance and investment products to unit trusts and international investments, pensions, provident funds and medical schemes.

The idea of setting people up in business for themselves in the financial services field, contracted to *Liberty Life* came about as a result of the increasingly competitive and sophisticated financial services environment and by anticipating future industry trends and legislation. Liberty has embarked on a strategy to develop its distribution channels by marketing their products in a unique and sophisticated manner aimed at clients at the upper end of the market. It felt that the industry needed rejuvenation and new blood. Only 10% of their existing franchisees have had experience in the financial services business – their success has been in recruiting franchisee candidates who bring with them managerial skills, business acumen and entrepreneurial flair learnt elsewhere. These talents form the basis on which the New Venture Academy then trains and hones the required skills to become a successful franchisee.

Given the high potential rewards in the industry and the low cost of entry, the selection process for a franchisee is intensive with a 5-stage process to establish potential and future performance. Once accepted, the New Venture Academy arm of *Liberty Life* offers franchisees and their consultants comprehensive training, full time for the first month and then part time at an advanced level for a further six months. Consultants may choose to specialise in fields such as individual portfolio planning, estate planning, retirement provisions, health care, investment planning and corporate benefits (i.e medical schemes, pension and provident funds).

Liberty Life believe that the future for the franchise is limitless with the market far from saturated. There is something in excess of R120 billion sitting in current accounts in South Africa, being under-utilised. Research shows that the A-B target income group is under-serviced, continues to grow (especially through upwardly mobile people from previously disadvantaged communities) and expresses a preference for one-to-one financial consultation of the highest professional level.

LIBERTY LIFE FRANCHISES – TRAINING YOU, FINANCING YOU, PUTTING YOU ON THE ROAD TO SUCCESS. FOR LIFE.

LIBERTY LIFE NEW VENTURE ACADEMY
Tel No; (011) 445-7004   Fax No: (011) 445-7005
e-mail: ross.marriner@mail.liberty.co.za

LIBERTY LIFE

MULTISERV - SERVICING THE MULTITUDES!

"Remember the good old days - 1969 to be exact - when rock 'n roll was King....stilettos were the rage .... and shoe repairs were done in a place called Multiserv in the OK Bazaars!"

To survive the highs and lows of thirty years in South Africa is no mean feat and *Multiserv* is indeed one of the few companies that can truly claim to have served the South African nation well – then and now. Shoe repairs and key cutting have been the core of their business and over those 30 years they built up a formidable company with close to 250 company owned outlets servicing in excess of 150,000 customers per month. Shoe repairs and key cutting remain the primary services but add-ons such as carpet cleaning rentals, apparel services and shoe/leather care products have widened the product base.

What *Multiserv* is doing for the "new" South Africa is also unmatched by anyone in business. In 1996 *Multiserv* made the transition from being a wholly owned corporate chain to the franchise network it is today. What sparked the change of strategy? Simply the fact that *Multiserv* offered the ideal vehicle to empower starter business people from all communities. And of course, franchising the concept offered the best of everything - from the franchisor point of view the owner/operator would improve service, shrinkage and growth whilst the entry cost, low risk factor and easy transfer of skills made it attractive to franchisees.

With *Multiserv's* wealth of expertise, both in management and store operators, the transition to franchising was far smoother than would be possible for any competitor starting from scratch. As a service company with over 250 stores employing over 400 people, mostly non white, *Multiserv* embarked on a programme of identifying potential entrepreneurs from within its ranks. Once identified these employees are groomed and guided in the mechanics of how to run their own businesses. Subject to a number of criteria being achieved in a company store, the opportunity to own their own business is the reward. Since converting to franchising in May 1997, over 20 employees have been put into their own businesses, with more in the process. With a total network of over 250 outlets, the potential and opportunity for franchise conversion is staggering.

The entire process has been a wonderful illustration of the power of franchising and empowerment at its best. Some stores that were doing fairly well before being franchised have since doubled their turnover. The new entrepreneurial vision in the company had an effect almost from the first day. At any moment, 40 or 50 prospective franchisees, some company employees and some new people, are either negotiating franchises, having their shops prepared for them or on the waiting list. The purchase price of existing stores ranges from R65,000 - R200,000, depending on the size of the store, its positioning and goodwill and the purchase price of a new store is R65,000 comprising the franchise fee of R25,000; R37,000 for machinery/tools/furniture & fittings and R3,000 for materials.

Multiserv is the franchise that works for everyone. High levels of education are not necessary; they look for motivated people who have a strong desire to succeed. He or she must be comfortable dealing with people and anyone with an inclination towards handwork will be able to do the actual shoe repairs after undergoing training in *Multiserv's* government registered training school. This transferal of skills is a unique way of ensuring that staff are highly skilled, professional craftsmen. They work with only the finest quality materials and their units are equipped with the most modern machinery and techniques. The support structure includes a comprehensive maintenance and shopfitting department, experienced in the maintenance of machinery, manufacture of fixtures and the layout of stores.

Despite the relatively low entry level cost of a *Multiserv* franchise, the affordability of buying a franchise still remains out of reach of the majority of South Africans. Although steps have been taken by the Government through specially appointed financing projects in conjunction with banks to assist small business in setting up, there are still numerous problems with financing and prospective entrepreneurs who would otherwise make excellent franchisees are often not given the chance to prove they can make it on their own. With a view to helping the many emerging entrepreneurs who approach *Multiserv* for a franchise, the company is introducing a totally unique alternative franchise option that is based on the "leasing" of the outlet from the franchisor at a fraction of the cost of purchasing a franchise. The risk, to a large extent, would be borne by *Multiserv* who would carry the costs of the equipment and its depreciation, with the franchisee operating independently but within the ambit of the franchise system.

It is such forward and lateral thinking that is making *Multiserv* one of the most exciting and progressive companies in South Africa today – exciting because it dares to challenge the status quo and progressive because it remains true to building a prosperous economy in South Africa through empowerment.

MULTISERV IS SUCCESSFUL FOR ONE SIMPLE REASON: THE WHEELS OF THE MASSES ARE ON THE SHOES OF THEIR FEET. AT ANY MOMENT THE SOLES OF THOUSANDS OF SHOES ARE BEING WORN AWAY!"

MULTISERV
Tel No: (011) 830-1722
Fax No: (011) 830-1783

NANDO'S IS LOOKING FOR THE HUNGRY FEW WHO AREN'T CHICKEN

"Nando's is not about chicken. It's never been just about chicken. It's about pride, passion, courage, integrity and, most of all, family."

This is the creed that has empowered *Nando's* to go from just one store to 140 stores in just over a decade. It is the inspiration that has grown the Nando's family from five to more than two thousand people over the same period. It is the motivation that has powered *Nando's* to sales of over R300 million per year. It is also the reason why *Nando's* has decided to venture where it has never been before with a bold new initiative.

We are passionate about this country. In fact, when we launched our first store in Rosettenville, Johannesburg, we called ourselves – "The Chicken for a new South Africa". And we believe we've lived up to that promise. We've created jobs. We've created wealth for our people. We've delighted hundreds of thousands of customers with our attitude and, of course, our food. Now we'd like to make even more of a difference.

We are going much, much further in our efforts to create opportunities, build wealth for the community and spread the *Nando's* magic. For the first time in our history, we want to franchise the *Nando's* concept to those champions who can help us make a difference to the community. At *Nando's* we believe that no matter how much we've done, we can always do more. That's why we are embarking on this journey. We want to reward those entrepreneurs who share our spirit of pride, contribution and courage with true ownership and independence. We want to be the inspiration that empowers people to achieve their highest aspirations. We want to be a sizzling role model for others.

We are looking for those people who have achieved the status of leaders in their community. We are looking for people of honour, integrity, strength and determination. We are looking for people who would be willing to give everything they have to make a success of their business and maximize their contribution to the community. We want those high performers who are willing to train hard, serve others well and have fun doing it.

At *Nando's* one of our core principles is that we always build a solid foundation ahead of growth. So if you've got the right stuff, we'll give you everything you need – the support, the marketing, the training, the infrastructure. We'll even assist you with the financing through a highly innovative agreement we've entered into with the IDC to help deserving candidates fund their dream.

Here's the deal: You give us your influence, your understanding of the community, and your commitment. We give you the Nando's recipe for success, wealth and joy. It's that simple – a partnership of equals where both partners make an acceptable return on sweat, energy and capital.

If you join *Nando's*, you will become what we call a *Nandocas*. A *Nandocas* is the name given to members of our family – the most special breed of people on the planet. One of the core beliefs of a *Nandocas* is that he knows he is only as good as the people around him. He's a team player on the dream team. And that's another reason why we are initiating the franchise strategy: We want people who are going to help inspire and excite *Nando's* to achieve world class standards out of Africa. We want people from all over the world to come to Soweto, Alexandria, Guguletu or Sharpville to discover the true meaning of excellence in food service. This is our dream. It is a big, bold, daring dream.But at *Nando's* we believe if you can dream it, you can do it. We've done it. Now we want to do even more. Because we know we can never stand still. Life at *Nando's* is a neverending adventure into the future!

So, do you think you could be a *Nandocas*? If you are genuinely the best of the best, we want your experience, your excitement, and your ideas. In return, we will help you build something beautiful from the ground up. We will help you make a real difference to your community. The two of us will create something that will make this country proud.

Call our executive in charge of franchising on (011) 887-7878 for more information on this exciting opportunity.

Nando's. Where you can taste your dream.

TAUNT YOUR TASTEBUDS

NIZAMS - CONTRIBUTING TO NATION BUILDING

Nizams reflects the true South Africa . . . the hustle and bustle of a colourful nation . . . the haggling and bargaining of the market place . . . and it is leading the field in empowering the man in the street!

Nizams is living proof that a solid business can survive the test of time and can adapt to the changing times. The *Nizams* success story spans 40 years and covers the entire spectrum of socio, political and economic changes in South Africa. Started 42 years ago as a family run general dealer store which catered to the wider population and stocking a diverse range of products at unbelievably low prices, the business grew over the years to include branches in Rustenburg, Witbank, Soweto, Katlehong and Daveyton which formed the test basis to their franchising strategy.

The family's unique understanding and grasp of their consumers' discriminating buying habits reflected in the success of their branches which proved successful beyond the directors' expectations, often tripling in size to accommodate the demand and success of the ventures. The idea of franchising the concept was considered and the directors began an intensive investigation into the feasibility of franchising. No expense was spared to tap into the resources of top franchise consultants, auditors and lawyers. The result was a blueprint for the successful franchising of the *Nizams* concept.

Eric Parker was one of the experts consulted by *Nizams* and he immediately recognised that the *Nizams* concept presented one of the most exciting and viable opportunities for significant black empowerment in the high gross end of the market. An essential factor to their success was that the informal sector of the economy they serviced was growing at three to four times the rate of the formal sector and that the spending power in these communities far outstripped that of their wealthier neighbours.

Launched in April 1998 at the FASA Expo, the concept broke new ground in franchising offering opportunities and filling a unique gap in retail and convenience store franchising. By mid 1999 – a little over a year – *Nizams* sold 30 franchises and today is well on the way to becoming the first truly South African retail franchise.

A traditional "bargain" store, with the hustle and bustle of women scratching for bargains, *Nizams* carries a carefully selected range of low cost, fast-selling goods which span housewares, appliances, clothing and footwear, haircare, cosmetics, perfumes, fancy goods, toys and novelties. Although the average *Nizams* consumer spends only R18-R20 per visit, the volumes are enormous with around 500 customers passing through each outlet daily, translating into minimum store turnovers of around R200,000 per month, and an average net profit of some R240,000 per annum. To date, all franchised outlets have consistently surpassed monthly targets by as much as 20%.

The total investment required to purchase a *Nizams* turn-key franchise is in the region of R350,000 to R450,000, depending on the size of the store with a management fee of 1% of gross monthly turnover and an advertising levy of two percent gross monthly turnover, royalties almost unheard of in the industry. When this is seen against an average mark-up of 35%, the franchisee is without doubt an extremely viable proposition.

Training of franchisees and store employees takes place at *Nizams* internal Academy of Learning which focuses on merchandising, marketing and motivation. All personnel are trained to understand customers' needs, to show them what they want and to make them feel comfortable without being pressured to buy.

A new development in the *Nizams* expansion strategy is the empowerment of the street hawker – clearly the most exciting niche market in the country. The potential for expansion in this area is mind-blowing and *Nizams* is breaking new ground in being the first retailer to sub-franchise to hawkers and is one of the only well organised hawking opportunities in the black market.

For just under R5,000, a hawker can purchase a fully equipped branded hawker trolley, complete with umbrella and uniform, move to an optimal location and hey presto! He's in business! For a small monthly membership fee, these sub-franchisees will receive discounted products from the local franchisee, trolley maintenance as well as ongoing training on what to merchandise in which season and at what prices. *Nizams* plans to have approximately 30 hawkers trading in the vicinity and under the auspices of each franchised store.

Experts in franchising have long held the view that the future in franchising is in the mass market and in the lower-entry franchise concepts. The empowerment and employment of the millions of previously disadvantaged is a reality of our times. The potential of each and every South African is there – all it needs is the determination and the opportunity which a franchise like *Nizams*, without question, offers.

NIZAMS! EMPOWERING THE NATION!

NIZAMS FRANCHISING
Tel No: (012) 328 2437
Fax No: (012) 328 2438
e-mail: www.nizams.co.za

PG AUTOGLASS - CRACKING THE FRANCHISE MOULD

If you're passionate about service . . . have the motivation to go it on your own . . . but want the safety net of a national leader . . . then PG Autoglass is for you!

What do you get when you take Belron International, an already global leader in the repair and replacement of automotive glass which is part of the PGSI Group with SAB Limited as its holding company and throw it the franchise challenge? You get success with a capital S and the complete metamorphosis of *PG Autoglass* in the last two years from a company comprising directly owned outlets into a soundly based, geographically diversified franchise group that has unlocked the potential of the entrepreneur.

More and more corporate conglomerates are looking to franchising to expand their markets and bring the stronger owner/operator success story into the equation. In late 1997 *PG Autoglass* opened 14 franchises simultaneously in the Eastern Cape. Barely a year later this figure stood at 38 countrywide and the plan is to open 60 franchises by the year 2000. It is indeed a tribute to the success of franchising when a corporate giant such as the PGSI Group can acknowledge that they see their franchise division as being the greatest growth area of the company and forecasting that their existing 40% market share and profitability will increase as a result of franchising.

What makes an already successful company with a solid brand name be so confident that by simply changing to the franchise formula, it can expect unprecedented growth? It's the merging of the entrepreneurship and local standing of small business people with the strength of a big name, say the directors of *PG Autoglass*. One could almost say business practices have come full circle since the Glass Merchandising Company, Jacobs & Dandor, to which the PG Group traces its origins, was established in 1897. In those days, it was a family business where one called on customers by bicycle. The manufacture of glass went through mammoth stages – the development of the first "safety glass" in 1929, Shatterprufe in 1939, Armourplate in 1948 and 100 years on PGSI celebrates its centenary as an international giant with the largest automotive repair and fitment business in the world.

But it is the "back to small business and personal service philosophy" that is winning the day and building brands these days. It is the combining of the strength of a world renowned company with its solid back up and business stability with the entrepreneurship and personal commitment of an owner/operator who brings with them a different level of experience and a more hands-on approach to building a business. *PG Autoglass* offers franchise opportunities to motivated self-starters from all walks of life who share the global company's values and ethics of service excellence, high technical excellence and ethical behaviour towards their customers and employees. *PG Autoglass* also offers existing businesses the opportunity of converting their businesses to a *PG Autoglass* franchise. They are guaranteed strong, well established branding, access to superior products, a reliable source of supply, technical training and information gleaned from a world-wide network of branches in 15 countries.

PG Autoglass has a three tiered entrance fee structure that accommodates the size of country and towns and addresses the car parq population that constitutes the franchise automotive glass potential. The establishment costs are also subject to whether the business is a new start up, an independent conversion or a purchase of a PG Autoglass fitment centre. A systems development fee determined by turnover volume as well as a management and marketing fee is levied to all franchisees and a suggested minimum 60 days start-up working capital is recommended for the ongoing operation.

PG Autoglass, over a period of 13 years has proved and refined the business, and allows franchisees to emulate their fine-tuned business formula. The acquired skills and standards of the franchisor are passed on to the franchisee and allows the franchisee access to the specialised and highly skilled knowledge of the head office management team whilst retaining his/her independence as a self employed operator.

Advantages of becoming a *PG Autoglass* Franchisee include access to a sophisticated IT system and strong relationships the company has with major insurance companies and fleet operators, together with the benefits of national and promotional budgets and of course the goodwill and awareness generated by the famous *PG Autoglass* reputation.

The strategic decision of *PG Autoglass* to franchise has generated a win-win scenario for themselves, their franchisees and the public alike. For PG Autoglass the vision for the future is filled with new challenges and opportunities, which as the leading automotive glass replacement and repair company in Africa, they will seize with enthusiasm and commitment. They will simultaneously and in a very focused way deliver the highest standard of service excellence to all future franchisees, whom they welcome to the bigger "PG" family.

PG AUTOGLASS . . . PUTTING THE "PERSONAL GAIN"INTO PRACTICE!

PG AUTOGLASS (PTY) LTD
Contact: Henk Myburgh
Tel No: (011) 928-2500
Fax No: (011) 974-7355
Dial Free: 0800 03 03 03

If you really want to do it, we'll help you do what you really want!

Introducing the Pick 'n Pay Franchise Information and Development Centre

Pick 'n Pay Franchise has been a remarkably successful business venture. Over the past five years, we have opened over 200 franchise stores under the following brands: *Pick 'n Pay Family Store, Rite Value and Score Franchise*. It has taken a massive amount of faith and hard work. It has also happened through the right people. Most of all, it has happened because the community has supported us wholeheartedly. Our continued success is totally dependent on the economic success of the people we serve. Now we want to give something back. We want to help the people who have helped us.

More and more, wealth creation and employment opportunities will not come from government or large corporations. They will come from new and emerging entrepreneurs. That's why we want to empower existing or aspiring entrepreneurs to develop their skills and expertise. We want to help grassroots businesspeople acquire the knowledge that will make them more successful. We want to transfer our knowledge and experience to those people who hold the future of their communities in their hands - the thousands of small businesspeople who trade everyday under the most challenging conditions.

Pick 'n Pay Franchise has established the *Pick 'n Pay Franchise Information and Development Centre* in Denver, Johannesburg. At our Information and Development Centre, we will be holding half day workshops for small businesspeople and aspiring entrepreneurs. These workshops will focus on the most important issues facing small business. The topics to be covered include:

- How to manage your emotions under stress
- How to program your mind for success
- How to achieve consistently high standards
- How to act and operate with confidence
- How to provide creative solutions to tough problems
- How to lead and inspire others
- How to keep going when the going gets tough
- How to write a business-plan for massive success
- How to market your business

- How to raise capital for your business
- How to control your cashflow
- How to choose and manage your staff
- How to create customer loyalty through outstanding customer service
- How to operate a successful business

We also want to help the youth of South Africa by helping them understand what it takes to be an entrepreneur. We want to champion entrepreneurship among young South Africans so they become job creators not just job seekers. That's why we will be reserving places on all our workshops for scholars and students.

These workshops will be facilitated by leading professionals as well as *Pick 'n Pay Franchise* staff and Franchisees who will share their real-life experience with delegates. These workshops are designed to transfer knowledge in a highly inspirational, straightforward and participative style. Whether you are a spaza owner in Soweto or a matriculant in Mondeor, you will find the Information and Development workshops exciting and enlightening.

The workshops will commence in August 1999. The cost is just R20 per delegate and there will be 120 delegates to each workshop. So not only will you learn valuable lessons on business but you will also get the opportunity to network with other likeminded individuals who want to be the most they can be.

The Information and Development Centre is a new initiative for *Pick 'n Pay Franchise*. It is another innovation from a group that has thrived on being first. Initially, these workshops will only take place in Gauteng. However, we will consider rolling out this concept nationally at a later stage. Furthermore, depending on the response, we envisage conducting workshops once every two months.

The Information and Development Centre and workshops are part of *Pick 'n Pay Franchise's* social responsibility program. They are our commitment to promoting entrepreneurship in South Africa. They are not an entry into *Pick 'n Pay* or its franchises. We are simply leveraging our experience, expertise and success to help deserving candidates achieve their dreams, goals and ambitions.

If you would like to know more about the Information and Development Centre and the workshops we offer, call Deirdre van Rooyen or Cindy Ellis on (011) 620-2569 or fax them on (011) 615-2300. Attendance will be strictly on a first book-first come basis.

Pick 'n Pay Franchise Information and Development Centre.

We'll help you turn on your power.

PLEASURE FOODS - PACKING A POWERFUL PUNCH

"In business focus is everything. Fast food is like fashion . . . you have to adjust the image continually to ensure that it does not lose its consumer appeal. The secret is to combine the two to have the winning formula."

It is this sort of progressive thinking and leadership that has put *Pleasure Foods* on the top of the heap as the largest franchisor of fast food brand names in South Africa. Their portfolio of companies - *Wimpy, Milky Lane, Juicy Lucy, Whistle Stop, Macmunch Fast Foods, Cantina Roosters and Market Cafe* have close to 500 franchised stores, with an annual turnover of more than R600 million. Since management bought the company from National Brands at the end of 1996, there has been a vibrant new sense of purpose and several of their brands have, in fact, taken on the fashion food challenge by hanging up the old image and bringing out a newer, trendier model. Throughout the *Pleasure Foods* group, brands have in the past few years been re-imaged and repositioned for the next millennium.

Service is the key at *Pleasure Foods* and working as a team is the first step in providing both an internal and external service. Specialists in training, marketing, information technology and computer systems, product development and the maintenance of high operating standards are involved in every aspect of the franchisee's business. The head office builds the brand, but the good franchisee builds the individual business.

A Fast food franchise is nothing more than the sum of its brands - The brands in the *Pleasure Foods* stable set them apart from their competitors and the success of those brands can be measured by the results. Each of the *Pleasure Foods* brands is unique, possesses its own culture and attracts a different type of franchisee. Only the principles of building a brand within the franchise system remain constant. The franchise opportunities in the *Pleasure Foods* stable include:

WIMPY
Since the day *Wimpy* opened thirty one years ago in the Murchies Passage arcade in Durban, it has become a household name in the South Africa and owning a *Wimpy* outlet is a highly rewarding option for prospective franchisees. It remains Pleasure Foods' flagship with close to 300 outlets spread across the country.

JUICY LUCY
Many will remember those heady days of the seventies, when the hippy era brought with it a return to the natural and those in the ethereal mood would head down to central Johannesburg to drink natural juices and eat yoghurt and beansprouts at the latest hot spot – *Juicy Lucy*. From that first store way back then to one of the first fast food outlets in the country to be listed on the JSE, *Juicy Lucy* retains its strong brand identity, high quality products, unique positioning, and incredibly loyal customers.

MILKY LANE

Whichever way you look at it – *Milky Lane* is a delicious option. Since its inception in 1958, in the era of the Chevy . . . the jukebox and the ice-cream parlour, Milky Lane has continued to leave its indelible and delicious mark on every generation that passes through its doors, pigs out on a sundae and grooves to the music videos. The total entertainment package that *Milky Lane* offers to both its franchisees and its customers is jam-packed with a bright new image and an "over the top" ice cream and eating out experience.

WHISTLE STOP

Being ten steps ahead of the pack is the rationale behind this exciting new concept that is the future in fast food. Re-examination of *Pleasure Foods* brands revealed that, in the case of the Golden Egg, it was better to reinvent than to revive. The result was a multi-million rand joint venture between *Pleasure Foods* , Shell SA and the franchisees. Golden Egg was relaunched as *Whistle Stop* - a new brand with a contemporary identity. Providing a wide range of eating options, including a sit down served fast food, a 24-hour take away and diner, *Whistle Stop* is ideally suited to the traveller.

MACMUNCH

One of the first "indigenous" franchise concepts to cater to the broader market with a diverse range of take-out options reflecting the colourful food tastes of our rainbow nation, *MacMunch* is in tune with the developing market offering empowerment through an affordable franchise concept but backed by the expertise and experience of the *Pleasure Foods* infrastructure.

CANTINA ROOSTERS

Cantina Roosters is positioned as a Mexican flavoured, rotisserie chicken fast food brand, with informal sit down dining as an option. It has strong family appeal and *Pleasure Food's* infra-structure and back-up should make this unique concept a winner.

MARKET CAFE

Pleasure Foods have followed the worldwide trend of developing a "shop-within-a-shop" with its exclusive deal with Pick 'n Pay and the introduction of the *Market Cafe* - an upmarket yet relaxed restaurant that offers a varied menu to suit all eating moments, from breakfast to dinner.

Pleasure Foods' advice to someone wanting to buy a franchise is: "Choose a credible company with which to link up, one with a proven track record of reliability and support to franchisees. But above all select a brand you can feel passionate about!" The range of cost-of-entry franchises offered by the *Pleasure Foods Group* is diverse - ranging from close to a million rand for a Drive-Thru to an affordable R175,000 for a take-out, depending on the investment requirements of each brand.

IF IT'S A PLEASURE FOODS FRANCHISE – WHAT A PLEASURE!

PLEASURE FOODS HEAD OFFICE

Tel No: (011) 803-7500   Fax No: (011) 803-7199

PLEASURE
FOODS

POSTNET - RESHAPING BUSINESS SERVICES!

Service . . . Convenience . . . Value . . . the Secret to Postnet's Success!

These three qualities have made *PostNet* one of the wonders of franchising in South Africa! The year was 1994, a turning point in the South African economic and political scene. The existing service of established facilities left much to be desired. Business services as such were non-existent, coupled with a fundamental lack of value in anything that had to do with basic communications. Four South African entrepreneurs took the plunge and challenged the status quo by daring to open up a business and communication services franchise – offering everyone from the housewife who needs stamps and photostating to the bigger business companies who need binding or courier services a fast, friendly and professional service. Within a short space of time, *PostNet* astounded its opposition and its critics by becoming a runaway success with over 155 franchised outlets countrywide.

PostNet is a perfect example of how quickly a brand can become an industry leader if it targets a niche market not previously supported with a high level of service, convenience and value. Recognising that the inefficiencies of the business communication services in South Africa provided an excellent opportunity for such an independent network of service providers, the group of four entrepreneurs opened their pilot operation as a part-time venture. Within six months they were so inundated with applications that they all threw their weight behind it full-time. Such a radical and risky venture into a business area so tightly controlled belies the directors' philosophy to "encourage and pursue ambitious ideas, but execute them in a conservative way." This cautionary approach continues to be a guiding principle with *PostNet* despite their phenomenal growth and expansion over the past 5 years.

PostNet is part of an International Franchise Corporation which began in the USA some 15 years ago. Based in Henderson, Nevada, the group's worldwide tally is more than 600 and their target – based on a steady annual growth rate maintained since 1993 – is to have a minimum of 1 000 stores opened by the year 2 000. At current expansion levels of a new shop every 10 days, this is well within the group's reach.

Rated by prominent business magazines in the United States among the top 50 business service franchises and one of the top 100 fastest-growing franchises in the world, the *PostNet* system provides an efficient, one-stop solution for a range of fast-paced global communication and business services. From courier and postal services, mailbox rentals, copying, lamination, printing and binding to fax services, computer services, greeting cards and ID photographs, the *PostNet* franchise network has built up a reputation of efficiency and reliability among the millions of people and companies around the world. Various other non-core products, that are consistent with the *PostNet* product mix, may be offered with the approval of *PostNet* Southern Africa.

PostNet offers two options to prospective owners of a *PostNet* centre.

-   a stand-alone *PostNet*, typically located in shopping malls of between 60 - 95sq. m
-   a *PostNet Express* – a store of between 30 - 35sq.m situated in a host location, e.g. supermarket, pharmacy etc.

Set up costs for both options varies according to the size of the store but a typical *PostNet* stand-alone store will cost in the region of R165,000.00 for set up costs, with an upfront franchise fee of R50,000.00 and monthly royalties of 6% for administrative royalties and 2% for advertising royalties. A *PostNet Express* will have set up costs of around R120,000.00, a franchise fee of R50,000.00 and monthly royalties of 6% for admin and 2% for advertising.

Committed to ensuring that each new franchisee succeeds, the franchise offers a comprehensive pre-and post-opening support service ranging from sourcing finance, lease negotiations, store build out, extensive classroom and practical training, operational support and toll free support for franchisees. This is augmented by fax updates and newsletters with the latest innovative ideas, success stories and current regional and national marketing strategies. A recently introduced intra-net service has proved a great success in on-line communications within the franchise group.

So effective has the *PostNet* concept been that the South African Post Office has acknowledged the role played by the expansion of this worldwide franchise network and has entered into an agreement with *PostNet* whereby approved *PostNet* franchisees will operate as retail business centres. The combined total of 2,450 Post Offices and 155 *PostNet* outlets will benefit the South African community with an extension of business centres. Another feather in the *PostNet* cap is its agreement with Standard Bank, one of the big four retail banks, to install business centres in about 80 of its bank branches. This heralds in a new era in the technology and distribution support arena which will see *PostNet*t provide e-commerce transaction facilities for on-line shopping.

There is no question that communications is the key to expansion in the new millennium. *PostNet*, with its worldwide innovation coupled with *service, convenience and value* gives you the unquestionable *PostNet* advantage!

IF IT'S GOT TO BE DONE . . .
GET TO POSTNET!

POSTNET S.A.
Tel No: (011) 805-0395
Fax No: (011) 805-3267
e-mail: http://www.postnet.co.za

GETTING INTO FOCUS WITH SPEC-SAVERS

"Spec-Savers has given opportunities to professionals and affordable eye-care to the nation."

Spec-Savers revolutionised the South African optical industry in May 1993 when it opted to franchise. It's quest was two-fold: Firstly, it wanted to offer professional optometrists the opportunity to own a top-notch professional optometric practice which gave excellent returns on their investment. Secondly, it wanted to make spectacles more affordable and so reach a wider spectrum of the population. Many people do not have medical aid and cannot afford a visit to the optometrist, nor glasses which could vastly improve their quality of life. The founders of *Spec-Savers* knew that, once the franchise concept had taken root, and with the resources and buying power of a formidable franchise group, they would be in a position to assist the man in the street to afford quality eye-care, whilst creating a growing and lasting asset for optometrists.

With over 90 franchises countrywide after 72 months, *Spec-Savers* has truly become the eye-care franchise to the nation. Part of the optometrist-owned FML Holdings Group, *Spec-Savers* opens up optometric care to income brackets as low as R400 per month through innovative credit deals. With the commitment of their franchisees, Spec-Savers optometrists are also doing their bit to help the less privileged in the country through clinics in lower income areas like Motherwell, Tembisa, Orange Farm and Vosloorus.

That's not to say that if you can afford it, you cannot find the best of the best at *Spec-Savers*. You want Gucci, Ray-Ban, Calvin Klein or Safilo – Spec-Savers have those too! They carry a top quality merchandise range and affordable eyewear to suit every pocket – all backed up by genuine guarantees. Well trained, friendly staff provide excellent customer service whilst qualified optometrists give top quality eyecare.

A *Spec-Savers* Franchise attracts qualified optometrists and opticians who opt to be part of this dynamic and expanding franchise. The purchase of a franchise includes the training and qualifying of capable and friendly front-line staff as Optical Assistants and Practice Managers. This entails distance training and attending modules that deal with the technical procedures and skills required by the operation as well as administrative, retail and selling training. Weekly in-store training covers current issues of relevance to the practices and follow-up training is conducted on a regular basis. Visits by the franchisor representatives serve to exchange views, give advice, deal with problems as well as monitor service standards, inspect the stores and introduce innovations in the methods and systems.

The marketing of the *Spec-Savers* brand is done on a national basis ensuring that there is uniformity in design and concept and that the public are given a strong brand identification. Market position and professional image is considered one of the key elements to the success of the brand and both national and regional advertising focuses on the service standards of *Spec-Savers* and more recently on the innovative credit options that make their eye-care service so affordable.

The franchise costs for a *Spec-Savers* outlet varies depending on the size, but the cost to set up an average 130sq.m practice complete with store design and layout and equipment, and including the R25,000 franchise fee is in the region of R550,000. A franchisee should ideally provide approximately R100,000 of their own capital prior to borrowings. Although financing is not available directly from the franchisor, assistance is given in obtaining the necessary financing. The licence fee is paid monthly as 6% of net turnover and adjusted annually according to gross profit achieved and a monthly marketing levy of 4% of net turnover is dedicated to the advertising fund.

The franchisor provides strong buying power, a powerful brand, a turn-key store-opening service – from the site inspection and lease negotiations to the design and fitting out of the store. Comprehensive computer training and support is given for the software before opening and a complete data conversion to comply with *Spec-Savers'* system is done. Central office staff co-ordinate and manage the opening of a new practice and the regional support co-ordinator of that region monitors the practice after opening.

The initial contract period is for five years with an option to renew the agreement for a further 5-year period. *Spec-Savers* is proud of the fact that since its first franchise practice opened in 1993, it has had a one hundred percent success rate and that independent practices that have converted to *Spec-Savers* have enjoyed well above average increases in turnover.

Franchising globally is expanding to include industries across the spectrum of business. *Spec-Savers* is leading the way in the franchising of professional services – and has done so in an innovative way, adapting it to South Africa's needs.

SPEC-SAVERS – THE AFFORDABLE OPTOMETRISTS

SPEC-SAVERS
Tel No: (041) 585-3351
Fax No: (041) 585-3282
e-mail: info@specsavers.co.za

SPUR STEAK RANCHES –
SIZZLING THE TASTEBUDS!

"Food is their passion . . . welcoming you to their home-from-home, their pleasure!"

Mention the word *"Spur"* to anyone - from the father who took his kids to the very first *Spur* that opened in 1967 in Newlands, Cape Town to a four year old who flips at the personal letter he gets from Spur on his birthday inviting him for a free meal and loads of fun – and they will all have some warm memory about their favourite Spur Steak Ranch. It might be the eager-to-please friendly and helpful staff who welcome you at the door; the rich, robust decor; the relaxing down-to-earth vibe or simply the mouth-watering smells, aromas, tastes and flavours that you *know* will give you satisfaction, every mouthful, every visit. *Spur* is a brand bursting with generosity for people who enjoy life one hundred and ten percent!

Food franchises come and go. Some are just passing fads. Others need to keep re-inventing themselves to stay in the game. *Spur Steak Ranches* are without doubt one of the only franchise groups that has stood the test of time, been around for 30 years and continue to make their customer their number one priority. The secret of their success? They, as a franchise group, practise what they preach. In the same way that their customers come into their *Spur Steak Ranches, Panarotti Pizza Pasta* outlets or *Busta's* take-aways to laugh, smile and have fun, so too is the *Spur* family exuberant, full of enthusiasm and helpful energy. Always on the go . . . Never slowing down . . . Their one purpose in life is to pamper the family, spoil the kids and give everyone a jolly good time and a tasty generous meal, time after time!

Behind the seeming ease with which *Spur* runs its operation, there is a passionate commitment to pursuing core values that are woven into everything they do. That passion is what they look for in their franchisees. *Spur* Head Office backs up their franchisees at all times to the full with regards leadership on a variety of fronts. Whether it is a new recipe or food item such as the new Lambone steak or through marketing; new decor or the latest account and cost control systems.

The primary value of a franchise lies in the quality of its product and service, the public's awareness of the brand name and the ability to deliver in a professional manner. The management of the *Spur Steak Ranches Group* ensures that a prospective franchisee is supported at all times and will, through service training and support, transfer those values to his franchised operation and ultimately his customers, every time.

The beauty of franchising is that it accentuates the positives and minimises the negatives of starting up a business. The concept of franchising is recognised as being the easiest, most secure manner for an entrepreneurial-minded individual to own and run his own business. The systems and comprehensive training plus the knowledge developed by the franchisor over the years, plus the support and backing of a financially sound franchise company is that rare combination that builds ongoing profitability and brand loyalty. With *Spur's* hands-on, "with-you-all-the-way" attitude there is no room for doubt . . . no hint of failure. The

Spur name, its image, consistently high standards of operation and the tried and tested *Spur* Business System in all three of their franchise concepts are all aspects of the recipe which reduce the risk factor of you going into business on your own.

Whether you're buying a *Spur Steak Ranch*, a *Panarottis Pizza Pasta* or a *Busta's Take-Away*, as a franchisee-in-training, you will be escorted through the complexities of owning-your-very-own-franchise business. From understanding the franchise agreement to compiling a detailed business plan; from training you and testing all your staff (yes, you will have to pass a final written exam!) on financial housekeeping, food purchasing, stock and cash control and budgeting to the selecting of staff and planning your launch. *Spur's* area management are always available through regular visits to assist and advise. But the bottom line is this: with *Spur's* over thirty years of experience, you know your franchise business is being given the best ever start-up.

Spur's franchise agreement runs for a period of ten years, with optional ten-year renewal periods. A licence fee of R80,000 is required which covers initial architect's fees, legal costs, training and other opening expenses. Royalties are calculated as a percentage of turnover (net of VAT) and are: 5% monthly franchise royalty and 4% monthly cooperative advertising levy which is spent on marketing the brand.

Costs vary considerably depending on the size and location of the franchise. A typical 220-seater *Spur Steak Ranch* would require a capital investment of approximately R1 300,000 of which R500,000 is in unencumbered cash and "own contribution cash" would be operating capital. *Panarottis Pizza Pasta* will require a capital investment of R735,000 (100 seater) of which R300,000 is unencumbered, plus royalties as per the Spur franchise agreement. A *Busta's* franchise would require a R380,000 (including licence fee) investment of which R150,000 is unencumbered.

What began in 1967 as a small, suburban steak ranch in Newlands, Cape Town is today South Africa's largest and most respected family sit-down restaurant group The Spur franchise has continued to grow, with 180 restaurants trading in the group's 31st year and an average 15 new Spur Steak ranches opening every year. *Panarottis Pizza Pasta* have over 50 franchises countrywide and *Busta's*, a new concept started in 1998 is set to be as big a hit.

SPUR IS BRAND POWERFUL, BURSTING WITH GENEROSITY, WITH A GREAT TASTE FOR LIFE!

SPUR STEAK RANCHES
Johannesburg - Tel No: (011) 803-4050
Fax No: (011) 803-5588
duncanw@spur.co.za
Cape Town - Tel No: (021) 462-1293
Fax No: (021) 461-6857

Appendix 1

Business Pre-opening Procedures Checklist

Task	Checked
1. **Prepare a Business Plan** - Whether finance needs to be raised or not as the document crystallises the nature of the business as well as the goals. A Business Plan focuses you attention on core issues, clarifies the direction the business is going to take and how you are going to get there.	
2. Decide on the business **target market** as well as the products and/or services to be offered.	
3. **Select a Site** - The site you select will depend on the nature of the business and should be easily accessed by the target market. Identify any competitors in the areas surrounding the chosen site. Meet with the landlord (if any) and enter into a lease negotiation before signing the lease document.	
4. Decide on the **name** of the business.	
5. **Pay Deposits** - Once the site for the business has been secured, pay all the necessary deposits, that is, water and electricity, rates and taxes etc and apply for services such as telephone/fax lines.	
6. Decide on a **business form and register** the business: a. Sole-proprietor - you do not need to register as a sole-proprietor thus business set-up costs are lower. b. Close Corporation - Reserve the name of the corporation on a CK7 form. The form must becompleted in triplicate and a R50 revenue stamp affixed to the original copy. Complete and submit form CK1 in triplicate and attach a R100 revenue stamp to the original copy. Forms CK1 and CK7 can be purchased in any major stationery store and revenue stamps may be purchased from the Post Office. A letter must be obtained	

Task	Checked
from the businesses elected accounting officer accepting his/her appointment as the CC's accounting officer and submitted with forms CK1 and CK7 to the Registrar of Close Corporations in Pretoria. Once approved by the Registrar, a CK number will be allocated. This number must appear on business forms, letters and invoices etc.	
7. Once the business site has been selected, visit the local council and request information pertaining to **compulsory registrations:** a. Registration of Employer for Pay As You Earn - If you have employees, you must complete and submit form IRP 101, Registration of Employer form to your local South African Revenue Services office. This must be done within 14 days of you becoming an employer. Once your business has been registered as an employer, the SARS will send you a supply of the following forms: RP 201 Monthly return of employee's tax deducted by the PAYE method. IRP 5 To completed by employer and that reflects the employees' annual earnings, pension, PAYE, Medical Aid, Unemployment Insurance Fund (UIF), etc., that will be deducted during the year. IRP 501 Used by the employer to reconcile the IRP 5s. IRP 10 Contains the tax deduction tables that are sent to all employers annually or whenever income tax rates are changed. *You DO NOT need to register for PAYE if:* Your staff members earn an annual salary of less than R 60,000. This amount changes from year to year. Make sure you check to see which is the current limit and whether or not you must register. If your employees earn less than R60 000 per annum, you will be required to deduct Standard Income Tax on Employees (SITE). SITE is calculated at the end of the tax period and NOT at the end of every pay period. Employees' tax, as per the tax tables in the IRP10	

Task	Checked
document, must be deducted during the course of the tax year. At the end of the tax period, you must calculate what portion of the employees' tax that you have already deducted represents SITE. Thus SITE is not a separate tax.	

b. Unemployment Insurance Fund (UIF) - If you employ staff, you must complete and submit the UIF form to the Department of Labour. This form covers employees earning up to R 82,000 per year. This figure changes from time to time, thus make sure that you check. Once you have registered you will receive forms UF 3 and UF 85.

UF 3 is the monthly return you must file for payment of UIF premiums.
UF 85 is the form used to register new employees. Existing UIF members should posses the UIF card which is normally blue. This card records the member's employment history.

c. Workmen's Compensation (WCA) - If you employ staff, you must complete and submit form WAs 2 to the Workmen's Compensation Commissioner in Pretoria. The WCA covers all employees earning up to R36,000.00 annual salary. However, this figure changes from time to time, so make sure that you check. Once your business is registered, you will receive the following forms:

WAs 8 This form is filed within 30 days of the financial year-end of the business. It reconciles the account.
WAs 6a This form shows the assessment made by the Commissioner for amounts of premium payable, less amounts paid in advance.

Note: IRP, UF and WAs are available at the local/regional Department of Labour office. Consult the Government Departments section of the telephone directory for contact details.

Task	Checked
8. Value Added Tax (VAT) - Businesses with sales of more than R 150,000 per year MUST register as a VAT vendor. Businesses with sales of less than R 150,000 can register on a voluntary basis. VAT must be paid over to the Receiver of Revenue on a monthly basis for businesses with sales of more than R 30 million per year or on request. A business that makes less than R30 million must pay VAT every two months. To register for VAT, you must complete and return form VAT 101. a. You collect VAT from your customers by adding 14% to the total amount they have purchased. b. You pay VAT every time you purchase supplies or pay for services. c. Every two months you are required to file form VAT 201 "Return for Remittance of Value Added Tax". Form VAT 201 basically takes the amount of VAT that you have collected and deducts the amount of VAT that you have paid. You must write a cheque to SARS if you collected more VAT than you have paid for the difference collected. Conversely, you will get a refund if you have paid more VAT than you have collected.	
9. Registering with the Regional Services Council - A business no longer requires a licence to trade. Instead you are to register the business with the local/regional Regional Services Council and are charged levies on either a monthly or annual basis. The amount payable is dependant on you turnover and the business' wages and salaries bill. a. Contact the local Regional Services Council and request that they forward form RSC. When you have completed the form it to the council. After approximately one month, a reference number will be assigned to the RSC1 and a certificate (a RSC2) will be issued in the name of the business as proof you are registered with the council.	

Task	Checked
b. Depending on the payment terms, you will receive an account (a RSC4) monthly or yearly and you must submit your Regional Services Council Levy along with the RSC4. c. Generally, the levy is calculated as 0.151620% of turnover and 0.379620% of total Salaries and Wages. These rates may vary from region to region and you should contact your local council to confirm these percentages as well as the procedure.	
10. **Opening a Cheque Account** - Open a bank account as soon as you have the close corporation (CK) number and/ or the name of the business entity. Apply for a cheque account by talking to either the branch bank manager or one of the consultants responsible for dealing with new business accounts. If you have been using a bank already, try that bank first. However, be open to check other banks that may offer you a better deal. Choose a bank/branch conveniently located near the business, shop around for the best value and service, check the bank fees charged by the banks for each cheque written and other transactions, Ask for overdraft facilities (this can take some time to be approved). You will need: • A valid ID document • Copies of forms CK 1 and CK 2 • A completed cheque account application which requires detailed financial information • If there is more than one owner, secure the other owner's signature, but it is preferable if all concerned are present. a. **Insuring the Business** - Ensure that you have sufficient cover on stock, equipment and the cash on hand. b. The best way to go about insuring the business is to approach a reputable insurance broker and request a	

Task	Checked
commercial quote on a short term policy. You should then "go shopping" for several comparative quotes. You must ensure that the quote covers your stock, all furnishings and equipment and the cash on hand. c. You may even want to ensure your business against public liability and sasria. If you are ensured against public liability and a customer slips on a wet floor in your store and injures him or herself, you will be covered. Likewise, if there is a public demonstration or march outside your store that results in a riot and your store is damaged, your store, stock and equipment will be covered. d. In some instances, the insurance company will not insure any cash in transit and it is advisable that you make use of a reputable security firm to transport your money to the bank. In other cases, and depending on the amount of cash you may have to hold in the business, the insurer may place a higher premium on cash.	
12. Rent a Post Office Box from you local Post Office and ensure that the postal address is recorded on all business stationery.	
13. Equip the Business Premises - Decide what furniture, fixtures and fittings the business requires to operate efficiently Obtain a list of suppliers by consulting the Yellow Pages and phone around for availability, price and after-sale service. Do NOT purchase equipment that is not vital to the operation of the business.	
14. Stationery and Supplies - Order/purchase office and stationery supplies. It is advisable that you do NOT go to the expense of having stationery printed when you first begin operating. This is an expense to the business that can be budgeted for at a later stage.	